Kings of Clubs

RONALD HEAGER

Kings of Clubs

STANLEY PAUL *London*

STANLEY PAUL & CO LTD
178–202 Great Portland Street, London W1

AN IMPRINT OF THE HUTCHINSON GROUP

London Melbourne Sydney
Auckland Bombay Toronto
Johannesburg New York

★

First published 1968

© Ronald Heager 1968

This book has been set in Times, printed in Great Britain on Antique Wove paper by Anchor Press, and bound by Wm. Brendon, both of Tiptree, Essex

For Gaye, My Golf Widow

Acknowledgment and thanks are made to the Editor of *Golf Monthly*, for use of material which appeared originally in that magazine

Contents

	Foreword	9
	Preface	11
1	Arnold Palmer	15
2	Gary Player	24
3	Peter Alliss	32
4	Hugh Boyle	41
5	Christy O'Connor	54
6	Dave Thomas	64
7	Michael Bonallack	74
8	Jimmy Hitchcock	82
9	Harold Henning	92
10	Bernard Hunt	103
11	Cobie Legrange	111
12	Neil Coles	119
13	Lionel Platts	127
14	Bruce Crampton	135
15	Leslie King	141
16	Tony Fisher	152

Illustrations

Arnold Palmer	*between pages*	24–25
Gary Player		24–25
Peter Alliss		24–25
Neil Coles		24–25
Bernard Hunt and Christy O'Connor		72–73
Dave Thomas and Jimmy Hitchcock		72–73
Michael Bonallack		72–73
Hugh Boyle		72–73
Lionel Platts		120–121
Harold Henning		120–121
Cobie Legrange and Bruce Crampton		120–121
Tony Fisher		120–121
Leslie King		120–121

Foreword

By DAVE THOMAS
(*Ryder Cup and Canada Cup international*)

There are more reasons than one why it gives me particular pleasure to write a foreword to this book by Ronald Heager. Not the least is that he is able to spread himself beyond the confines of the daily newspaper in which his golf writing is so widely known. Golfers in general, and we professionals in particular, are rarely satisfied with the space our game receives in the daily newspapers. No doubt the writers feel the same.

Over the years Ronald has become more than just a day-to-day reporter of the game. He has become a friend of it in all its aspects. I know him to be a confessed addict so far as playing the game is concerned, and in consequence he takes a deep interest in all the problems of the player in top tournament golf. He serves the game as secretary of the golf writers. There is little doubt he is doing a job he loves.

As a result of all this he has a good understanding of all that goes on in big golf, not only on the surface but, perhaps more important, behind the scenes as well. It is this sympathetic yet knowledgeable feeling for golf that is so much welcomed by the tournament player, who becomes something of a public figure in the increasingly popular spectator sport of golf. We find nothing more irritating and exasperating then the comments of the ill-informed, the shallow criticisms of those who only touch the surface of their subject.

In this book the author is able to draw on many years of experience as an observer of competitive golf on both sides of the Atlantic. This background enables him to write intimately and with authority about the leading figures in the game today. I like the idea of this collection of profiles and interviews presented as a book. There are many golf instructional books, a few biographies, but not enough about the people in golf appears in book form. The author here gets players talking about themselves and the game of golf. He has the knack of drawing them out. This is a good thing in that it portrays personalities through their own thoughts, and so must give the on-lookers a better understanding of the players and their problems. People see you at the top, but do not realise what you have done to get there. This book is big golf on the inside.

I welcome among the subjects several players lesser known than Arnold Palmer and Gary Player, but who in their way are just as important to golf, and have just as interesting a story to tell. It is pleasing to find this recognition given to the teaching specialist Leslie King, and my own former assistant at Sudbury, Tony Fisher, who has carved out for himself the unique role of golf's ambassador-extraordinary to Nigeria. You will find yourself dipping into this book again and again, for between the lines there is quite a lot said that could improve your game.

Dunham Forest Golf Club
Altrincham, Cheshire *October, 1967*

Preface

Twenty years of golf reporting is a lot of golf shots. It is also a lot of people. And people in golf are what this book is about. To me the players, as much as the play, are the thing. This is not to clamber on a limb and assert the performers are greater than the game. Golf has lived 500 years. It will live another 500, and longer—though it is a tremendous relief to know that I shall not be around to comment on the form it takes in the year A.D. 2468.

The extreme physical pleasures of playing the game are not lost upon me. I have split a fairway with a drive well past the 200-yard marker, felt the sweet click of a perfectly timed big iron shot, holed from a bunker, once sank a putt of 25 yards—all paced—and been ten inches off a hole-in-one. But the point is, I have seen all these things done better, and intentionally, by experts.

The historic aura of St. Andrews. A russet October morning at Gleneagles. The manicured and man-made perfection of courses in the Californian desert. These and a hundred other golfing shrines are locked in memory. And better, they are peopled by the giants of our age. Ben Hogan at Wentworth. Dai Rees at Lindrick. Peter Thomson at Royal Birkdale. Sam Snead in Palm Desert. Gary Player and Jack Nicklaus at Muirfield. Nicklaus again at Augusta, Georgia, in springtime.

Alongside the masters marched their frustrated rivals. There is a small host of these. There has to be, for what honour would remain for the champions if there was no one around to beat? So all grades and manner of golfers have their part. None less than the teaching professionals, often graduates of the tournament ranks. Their responsibility in unravelling the sweet mysteries of the game for others is as high as that of any of the gladiators who entertain in tournaments.

All have come my way—thanks to a thousand-and-one assignments for the sports pages of the *Daily Express*. Fleet Street has been my passport to faraway golf places which are but strange-sounding names to all but the international jet-set of tournament golf, and the well-breeched few who can pay to follow the sun. But the headlines limelighting who won this £1000 or that £10,000 event, who broke which course record or what rule of golf, are but the glamorous tip of the iceberg. What of the hidden nine-tenths? What of the heartbreaks, the prizes that got away, the long slog to Successville? The answers to these questions need depth. And a certain amount of digging. I began to seek and set down the stories behind the headlines for *Golf Monthly* magazine some ten years ago. The work yielded fascinating interviews, many lasting friendships, a deeper understanding of what makes a top golfer tick—and the material for this book.

Arnold Palmer is looked at through the eyes of his opponents. Gary Player talks of his Grand Slam of great championships—and 'the morning after'. There are the success stories of Michael Bonallack, Bernard Hunt and Neil Coles; and the frustrations behind the careers of Peter Alliss, Dave Thomas, and Jimmy Hitchcock. Hugh Boyle and Lionel Platts each tell of a long apprenticeship before their breakthrough in tournaments. The consistent Open Championship record of Christy O'Connor is put under the microscope. Overseas players Harold Henning, Bruce Crampton and Cobie Legrange point the way to winning golf all round the world. Teaching specialist Leslie King and unique club professional Tony Fisher call the tune of other people's swings, but still they come out of the same bag.

Kings of Clubs, all of them.

RONALD HEAGER

London, 1967

I

Arnold Palmer

MANY British Ryder Cup players have stood on the first tee with a match against Arnold Palmer ahead of them. The battlegrounds have been Royal Lytham St. Annes, East Lake Country Club, Atlanta, Georgia, Royal Birkdale and Houston in Texas. The matches have been singles, foursomes, fourballs. Palmer has had some 20 encounters in the Ryder Cup series. He has not always won. But never has one of his matches been anything short of a dramatic, thrill-charged, crowd-pleasing round of golf.

What accounts for the dynamic American's greatness as a golfer, his magnetism as a man? Ask a hundred people and you would get a hundred answers. I have gone part of the way by putting these two questions to some of the men who have met Palmer in Ryder Cup warfare. The comments of Britain's great players are fascinating and illuminating. They are flattering and penetrating; revealing and amusing. But they are not complete. Palmer as a subject is inexhaustible. As exciting, as unpredictable, as his next round of golf.

My own memories of him go back to June 1960, when he made his first appearance in Europe in the Canada Cup matches at Portmarnock. He had just won the U.S. Masters and Open championships. His appetite for a modern times 'Grand Slam' had been whetted. That in itself gave excitement to the man. He stayed for his first British Open, the 'Centenary' in which Australia's Kel Nagle pushed him into second place. Arnold came back—to win at Royal Birkdale and at Troon. And to lose at Royal Lytham. In defeat Palmer was still great. He walked off the last green with a score that put him at the back of the field, 294—as it turned out 17 shots behind Bob Charles and Phil Rodgers, who tied for first place. But the defending champion still managed to grin as he walked off the 18th green and say with a look at an adjacent tubular steel TV tower: 'Is this where you hang yourself?' A moment in big-time sport to cherish.

The closer you get to Palmer the more you like and admire him. For his wonderful sense of humour. Among the first words I heard him speak were answers to questions after his first practice round at Portmarnock. Did he like the smaller British ball? 'Sure. It makes the hole look bigger,' he replied. These bright unscripted gems have flowed from him ever since.

Then there is his monumental tolerance. With the galleries, the autograph chasers, above all with newspapermen. No question is too damn-fool for Arnie. No intrusion too great—as I found when I asked the great man to pose for a picture when stretched on his hotel room bed beneath a heat-treatment lamp. Remember the drama of 'The Back' at Palmer's Troon Open?

You bracket him high for these qualities of fun and never getting high-hat despite success and riches. You cherish and thrill to his achievments and his super golf shots. You marvel at his crowd magnetism—and you understand it.

But there are still more aspects of Arnie. An underlying streak of humility towards the game of golf which cuts across his brutal, cave-man attitude of attack. His warmth in relations with his fellows. And the especial depth of his partnership with Winnie, his wife. Winnie is the unknown soldier in the ranks of 'Arnie's Army', without privilege, without escort, but ever there with the reassuring glance or touch if her gladiator should require it.

One pair of eyes is not sufficient to obtain the full image of a great man. That is why I asked some of Arnold's rivals how they see him. Here then is what they say:

PETER ALLISS: He's exciting. He's slim and athletic. He looks rather fierce. He looks trim. Nicklaus is a great player but he looks soft by comparison, somehow. Jack doesn't walk like an athlete. I think everything Palmer does is rather electrifying. The way he jerks his head and walks quickly; everything's on the move all the time. He looks very fit. He hits the ball hard. He's got all the body actions after he's hit the ball. He looks well trained. He's like a well-trained actor, if you like. Some actors are more flamboyant than others and I think that he's an ace man at his trade and he has all the little flamboyant tricks that make him a crowd-pleaser.

He uses the crowd as a spur. They've come to watch him play and he'll show them some good stuff. They're not his enemies. They're there to find his ball and share all his good shots and worry his enemies. He looks upon them as such. In this country, playing with him, everyone was on my side. Over there everyone was on his side. Spectators are noisier over there. They say 'Go get him, Arnie', and 'You've got him now, Arn!' Things like that. Whereas over here they say 'Well done, Alliss.'

His greatness is golf? He's just a very good player. He's perhaps not technically as correct as some others... not as Snead. You wouldn't call Palmer a textbook man. He seems to hit so many shots hard and his body seems to be out of position a lot of the time. But he manages to get the clubhead back to the ball square. He gives the impression of power; such live power, I think.

BERNARD HUNT: Success. I would say success is the big thing about Palmer. I think everybody expects him to win, and that's why they go to watch him play. He's one of the men that, as Peter Alliss said, gets his momentum from the crowd willing and wishing him. I think that if he's playing well, the more the crowd cheer him on the more things he'll try to do. And, of course, when a man has spent all his golfing life as he has, attacking the course, whatever course it is, if he gets things going for him he'll attack all the way and do some of the most fantastic things. He'll try impossible recovery shots and get away with them. Things like that.

Any winner is exciting. And any man who has Palmer's record is exciting. Whether he's playing well or not he'll still draw the crowd. He'll still play those difficult shots, the attacking game. Everyone admires it, the fact that he tries it. They like to go and see him.

It's the same in this country if you're watching Harry Weetman. If you're out with Weetman everybody is wanting him to hit the impossible shots all the time. They go 'O-o-o-h' when he hits it. They do the same with Palmer. But you can be playing with Weetman and hit the ball the same distance with a bit of luck. But there's no 'Oooh' because there's no effort in it as they see it. Palmer throws himself at it. He appears to have hit a good shot. That's what people want to see.

His method: He knows what he's doing and that's good enough. He's one of the best putters in the business. That's the strength in his game. Plus his great physical strength.

TOM HALIBURTON: Nothing but the best . . . in all departments. As a man and as a player. He's got this delightful personality and everybody feels that he is a kind hearted, nice man. They sort of like him. A form of semi-love develops.

He seems to have this fair, open face. He looks as if he'd never do anything underhand. Yet he's a golfing tiger. This is the split personality of Palmer. He's so nice to everybody, as you Press boys know. It's always 'Come in, boys, have a seat'. Tolerant is the word. When anybody speaks to him he would never be sharp or aggressive.

I've seen better strikers, but he has a tremendous aggressive spirit, a will to succeed. British golfers like Abe Mitchell struck the ball far better, but Palmer has this tremendous will to get the ball into the hole.

In our match at Lytham he was terribly nice to me. He wished me good luck on the first tee. He said 'Good shot' if I played a good shot. Or 'That was a good hole, that was a grand second you hit there', as we walked to the next tee. Something like this, you see. I couldn't say anything wrong about Palmer.

DAI REES: Arnie 'gets' the galleries because he is so much in command of the situation. That pleases the crowd enormously. And his figures, obviously, are a big draw. He talks to the crowd, too, about the shots, and to his caddie. They find that interesting. You might say he's almost like Rees in that respect!

As a golfer, his strength—he's so physically strong—helps to make him great. Plus the fact that he has dedicated himself so much to the game and perfected a scoring method. Sheer hard work, I would say, put him in the class he is. Sheer hard work....

BRIAN HUGGETT: Concentration. Determination. These are the things that make Palmer the great player he is. You get the impression that if he has got a five-iron shot to hole he will hole it. And there is his putting... he appears to will the putts in. When he gets down to play a shot you can feel the concentration he is putting into it. His temperament makes him a great golfer.

He is a great sportsman, too. I'll never forget his bearing

when George Will and I played him and Johnny Pott in the opening foursomes of the Ryder Cup at Atlanta and managed to beat them. Not a sign of resentment or irritation and his congratulations were utterly sincere. After all, he was captaining the American side for the first time and this was the very first match. On top of that George and I were the two 'kids' of the British side—the youngest. Who knows, we might have been setting the pattern for a shock defeat of the United States! He took the result wonderfully. Then he came out in the afternoon with Billy Casper and beat us.

He gives the crowd such value by making the game look so hard. He thunders the ball and you can almost see the tee shaking when he has driven off! Then there is that big, high finish of his. That impresses the fans. I noticed at Atlanta that he walked down the sides of the fairways, close to the galleries behind the ropes, as if to keep in touch, to keep close to them. It all added to their enjoyment, increased the good value he gives. There is nothing aloof or remote about him.

CHRISTY O'CONNOR: Palmer's appeal is like that the Beatles first had. They were the greatest thing in show business. He is the greatest in sport. Arnie's Army is not far away from the screaming teenagers. The public in America have to have idols. They have ever since Jack Dempsey and Babe Ruth, Walter Hagen and Bobby Jones. Gary Player has his 'army' too. You see them out there with Gary Player slogans on their tee-shirts. Palmer pleases the galleries because he makes his golf look so good. Every shot he hits is a spectacle. He appears to hit the ball so hard, though quite a lot of players make the ball go further. But they don't put in anything like the *obvious* effort that he does.

His greatness? As I see it, that's life—there must be some people who have got a little more than others.

Arnie has this. Also he is so strong, just as Jack Nicklaus is. This gives them their super hand control.

GEORGE WILL: Palmer seems to hypnotise his galleries. He gets them all on his side, and they're out there yelling 'Come on, Arnie!' 'Give us a bird, Arnie!' There's no doubt this is an enormous help to him. He seems inspired by it all. What gets the fans is that Arnie is such an attacking player. I played with him at Rancho in Los Angeles when he had 12 in one hole. He flashed three shots out of bounds. There was no question of caution or compromise. He tried the same attacking shot every time. Palmer in this attacking vein is like a rhino charging—nothing can deflect him.

Nicklaus is a better player, but the crowd—and I agree with them—would rather watch Palmer. Nicklaus is so long, so straight, so accurate. The only stroke you have to watch with Jack is his putt. If it goes in it's a birdie. It it doesn't it's a par. Palmer is so different. He gets into trouble. Then he does the impossible, and gets out of it. As an opponent, I can only say he is a fine gentleman. Yes, he is a paradox. So fierce with a golf ball, so gentle as a man.

DAVE THOMAS: When you stand on the tee with Arnold you are thinking about his reputation. He is the No. 1. You know that you can't afford to drop a single loose shot. But even if you don't he still beats you. When Brian Huggett and I met him in the fourball matches at Atlanta he and Dow Finsterwald had a better ball of 29 for the outward half. Palmer had a personal 32. He is exciting as a player and as a man. You're always wondering what's going to happen next. Nothing appears impossible. The crowd is always urging him to do the impossible.

During a recent tour in the States the boys over there were telling me they think the crowd are a terrific help to him. You cannot put it into shots, but it must amount to a good number in the course of a year. The sheer weight of his crowds stop his bad shots from producing bad results. Two or three times I've seen his ball bounce off the crowd into playable lies.

As a golfer his powers of recovery, the way he plays the trouble shots, and his fantastic chipping and putting make him what he is. It's not the way he swings a golf club, not his style.

KEN BOUSFIELD: I remember Palmer at Lytham most of all for his terrific hitting against Dai Rees, who was then hitting the ball as far as ever he had. Dai and I lost two and one against Palmer and Billy Casper, but I still think it was a match that could have gone either way. The turning point was at the long sixth where they were in the rough all the way and Casper chipped in for a four. Instead of being all square we were two down.

Palmer is great, but not as great as Ben Hogan. I played against Hogan with Fred Daly at Pinehurst. Ben and Jimmy Demaret, his partner, were something much harder to beat. Hogan's marvellous accuracy makes him the greatest in my book. He was never in trouble.

Palmer's strength is his ability to bang his way out of trouble. He is, of course, one of the greatest putters of all time, a much better putter than Hogan. His terrific desire to win everything makes him the figure he is. The crowds love him because he is such an attacking player.

NEIL COLES: Christy O'Connor and I ran into an outward of 29 when we played Palmer and Finsterwald in the afternoon fourball series at Atlanta. There's no doubt he is good, but he does not impress me so much as Hogan did. I was more awestricken when I first saw Hogan play than ever I have been by Palmer. Sheer positioning of the ball puts Hogan ahead as a golfer. He was further ahead of his contemporaries than Palmer. He seemed able to win when he wanted to win more frequently than Arnold, though it's only fair to say competition is probably tougher now than it was when Hogan was at his peak. Palmer has terrific concentration, but to look at he is just a big slasher. Though he is so brutal to a golf ball, I do not think of him as a colourful player in the way Chi Chi Rodriguez or Doug Sanders are.

JOHN PANTON: As a shot-maker, Palmer is not as good as Hogan, Nelson or Snead. But there are so many other qualities that make him a great player. His power, his temperament, his determination, and a masterly short game. He is a wonderful putter, one of the best of all time.

The crowds love him because they get such a thrill seeing someone hit the ball off the tee like he does, crunching his woods and crushing his iron shots. He has the same appeal as Harry Weetman over here. Harry attempts the impossible and often achieves it. And this is bound to be crowd-pleasing stuff. On top of all that, Palmer is always so pleasant, so friendly. His relations with the fans are everything they should be.

2

Gary Player

THERE was a time when an interview at the Savoy Hotel meant an appointment with a rajah from India, a baron of industry or an aristocrat of the world of entertainment. Today this is the social bracket of Gary Player, for it was in a fifth-floor suite reached along an avenue of thickly carpeted corridors that I kept a date with the 'Grand Slam' golfing monarch from Johannesburg. He was passing through London after having flown over the Pole on the way home from the 1966 Canada Cup in Tokyo. He had a week's business to settle in the capital. His wife Vivienne had flown some 6,000 miles north from Johannesburg to shorten the absence from her husband. Both had still to endure the parting from their young family of Jennifer (then 7), Mark (5), Wayne (4), Michelle (3), Teresa (rising 2).

Gary and Vivienne greeted their numerous callers in a spacious room with a sweeping view of the Thames below it. Even out of golfing uniform the little Master was clad in black, informally in slacks and cardigan. His presence in London was to deal with business and literary affairs. He had appointments with sponsors, photographers, publishers, authors, his London agent. One of the projects was the promotion of wool—a finger in Britain's export drive. He spoke of a transatlantic telephone call to his manager Mark McCormack in America the previous

Arnold Palmer (U.S.A.). Exciting and athletic. Powerful and dramatic. The very fairways shake at his shots

Gary Player (South Africa). At 30 all peaks of championship golf had been scaled by the little 'Man in Black'

eter Alliss (Parkstone). Classical method has yielded more
1en ten years at the top on the tournament trail

Neil Coles (Coombe Hill). Quiet manner and thinning hair mask the huge talent of one of Britain's modern masters

evening as you and I would of a three-minute local call.

Gary was working at the business of being one of the most celebrated sportsmen of his age. Appearances suggested he was enjoying it. His last morning in London included dates in Jermyn Street to order hand-made shirts and shoes. Vivienne had not been idle. Her calls took in the royal antique dealer's establishment in Bond Street. The Players after a decade of dedication to success in golf were taking 'time off to smell the flowers', as the great Walter Hagen put it. 'London is now my favourite town. It's great to have time to really look at it after all the times I have simply seen only the airport and a couple of golf courses,' enthused Gary.

You could talk a night away with Gary Player. He has so much to offer on the subject of golf. And his eagerness to learn about life makes him plus four as a listener, too. So I had to choose my brief and get Gary to concentrate on just one aspect of his eventful career. I was curious about the year 1966 in the life of Gary Player, the one after the 'Grand Slam' year, a kind of 'morning after the night before'. Predictably, it was not a twelvemonth of such outstanding achievement. In '65 Gary won the U.S. Open, to complete his collection of the four major titles of modern golf. He added the Opens of South Africa and Australia, the Canada Cup individual trophy and the team title with Harold Henning, America's World Series of Golf, and in Britain the Piccadilly Match Play, after that homeric recovery from seven down against the late Tony Lema.

In '66 just the South African Open and the Piccadilly titles were retained.

Gary, the most articulate of athletes, straight away gave a most pungent summary of the situation.

'Nineteen-sixty-five was a hard year to follow. You

wouldn't dare write a film script including all the successes I had that year. Nobody would believe it,' he said.

'I wouldn't say 1966 has been a bad year. I played five tournaments in South Africa and won three. In America I played only 11 tournaments, but still won $28,000. I was fourth in the British Open, sixth in the Australian, I won the Piccadilly, and Harold and I were second in the Canada Cup. Whatever I did had to look worse than 1965. That was exceptional. Winning the Piccadilly again, and beating Neil Coles, Arnold [Palmer] and Jack [Nicklaus] to do it, made 1966 a nice year.'

Vivienne Player, meanwhile, had been an attentive listener. As daughter of veteran South African pro Jock Verwey and sister of tournament player Bobby, she has a true professional outlook. She played to around two handicap before her marriage. Further, before her young family's increasing demands she toured the American circuit with Gary full-time. Vivienne, I recall, brought newly-born Jennifer to the British Open triumph of 1959, and still makes it her duty to be present at most of Gary's major championship bids. It was with authority, then, that she spoke of Gary's 1966 campaign. Vivienne said:

'Gary did not give himself a chance, Besides all the new promotional activities arising from 1965, he was always flying home to the farm. He went three separate times to America to play in 11 tournaments. That is no way to do well over there. When he was in America he was not playing all the time. He was making store appearances, attending dinners and other functions, and fulfilling a packed programme of promotional activities as the U.S. Open champion.'

Gary told us himself before the Open championship at Muirfield that immediately preceding the American Open he made 15 appearances in department stores in five days in five different cities. These are not excuses.

Simply facts. He arrived early in Scotland for the British Open and spent a holiday at Gleneagles Hotel in his programme of acclimatising for Muirfield. Still he went away a disappointed golfer. His game was not sharp enough. He used 70 putts in the first two days. Iron shots were going astray. He said he played 'a lot of rubbish'.

When Gary was at Muirfield I asked him how his plan to cut down his tournament schedule was working out. He had announced after winning the 1965 Piccadilly that, with all the peaks scaled, he would restrict his appearances, give up the nomadic touring pro's life to some degree, devote more of his time to family, farming, and his youth welfare activities. He replied at that time, 'I don't know yet if you can still win tournaments when you don't play all the time. I am still experimenting.'

Now Gary's golfing year was over. Four months had gone by, and I put the question again. He called the experimental season a 'nice year'. But it was quite obvious that it had not been a completely satisfying one. Perhaps it had to be that way after a man had reached the golfing summit of the modern 'Grand Slam'. There has to be a recession. A retrenchment. Exploitation of the situation. Time, even, 'to smell the flowers'. Player and his advisers are already planning better things than living upon the glory of 1965. There will be changes. Tournaments will return to first priority. The celebration party is over. There were many signs of this in what Gary had to tell me. Knowledge of the man reinforces the belief. First of all there is his love of golf, then the zest for competition, appetite for any challenge, and abounding physical fitness and capacity. The sweet life at the top has not blunted any of these success factors in the make-up of Gary Player. And when he talked of the years to come every point he made signposted the way ahead.

'I feel in my heart I will win a lot more tournaments,'

said the man who passed his 31st birthday on November 1st, 1966. 'There must be a way you can still win without playing 30 or 40 tournaments a year. Sam Snead found the answer. Between the ages of 40 and 50 he began to pick his tournaments, but he was still a winner. Sam practises and plays every day of his life. That is why he can come along and still put up a good show, even win. As long as you keep the feel of the game in friendly non-tournament golf I believe you can still come out and do well. In the past year, I must confess, I became so interested in work on my farm that I just forgot about golf altogether. I spent a lot of time there and did not touch a golf club.

'In future it is going to be different. I have had constructed on the farm an area 300 yards by 30 yards, which is being laid out as a driving hole. I am having a putting green made also. When I am there I will be able to put in at least an hour a day practice. This will make all the difference.'

Different, too, will be the planning of Gary's tournament play on the one hand and on the other his promotional appearances and exhibition and television golf. He said: 'When Jennifer's school term ends early in December we will all move up to Magoembas Kloof, my farm about 200 miles north of Johannesburg. There I'll spend six weeks. My first trip to America will be early in the year to attend to business commitments and get as many of them out of the way as I can so that I can concentrate on my golf.'

Gary went to a table and picked up a couple of sheets of foolscap and began to catalogue this pre-tournament schedule. 'Twelve store appearances, four appearances at dinners and talks for my United Fruit Company promotion, three appearances for the shirts I endorse, three for slacks, two for a finance company, my commitments at the Castle Harbour Golf Club in Bermuda, eight exhibitions and an unspecified number of TV matches.

'The idea is to eliminate this kind of work from the periods I am playing in tournaments. I found the two things did not mix. Obviously they cannot. I shall do five tournaments on my first playing visit to the States. This will include the Masters at Augusta. I will do some more business at the end of this trip and then return home for a month.

'I'll go over again for a further four or five tournaments as the build up to the U.S. Open.

'Then will come the British Open. I will arrive at least a week beforehand. As I said at Muirfield, if you cannot give at least a week to acclimatisation and practice for the British Open it is not worth coming at all. The circumstances would have to be really exceptional for me to appear in the British without a week's preparation. I intend to compete in the British Open as long as I continue to play tournament golf.'

That will be the Player pattern of the future. Gary's major targets are the U.S. Masters, the U.S. Open and the British Open. He says:

'If you win one major championship then you can say you have had a great year. One of those is worth winning 20 other tournaments.'

It was at the end of the 'Golden Year' of 1965 that Gary retired to meditate in the wide peaceful 900 acres of Magoembas Kloof upon the pattern of his future. The non-stop round of jet planes, hotel rooms and suitcase existence had to stop. But there was so much good golf left in Gary. A decade at the top, at least. A formula of compromise had to be found. An essential ingredient was a haven from the enervating pace of being a hero in a hero-worshipping world. Gary looked at Snead, at his great contemporaries, Arnold Palmer and Jack Nicklaus.

He learned from the manner Snead paced himself. From the pattern of Nicklaus's life—the escape hole of a Florida home, the deep-sea fishing. Most of all he learned from Palmer.

'What success did to Arnold is the biggest warning I ever had,' said Gary. 'Involvement in business really hurt his game. Not having any real hobby, he could not get away from it all. He'd take time off and go home, but he never really escaped from golf and people and the hero-worship. This is terribly important, to get away.

'I've got myself something better than any golfer ever had. My farm. There I really escape from the world. My nearest neighbour is two miles away. It is four hours from Johannesburg. The telephone is shared on a party line of eight, so everyone gives up trying to reach me by phone.'

From this base Gary came and conquered at Wentworth for the second successive year. From it he will launch his future campaigns. He will relax there, and at the same time keep golfing hand and eye in.

Another aspect of the 1966 recession was that Player dropped the weight training which played such a tremendous part in 1965. He gradually built up the old schedule again, with emphasis on tremendous leg power. This he did in '65 by a squatting routine with 250 lb. on his shoulders, and an occasional 300 lb., straightening up 15 times, and repeating the medicine three times daily. 'Don't let anyone tell you weight training and golf don't mix,' said Gary emphatically. 'I was doing this routine during the U.S. Open at St. Louis when I won. I gave up only because of medical advice when I had an injured back and high uric acid. Then I got a bit lazy about it, but I have to get it going again.

'I have started already, in fact. If I was in London long enough I would look round for a gymnasium. Meanwhile I am running up and down the stairs to the fifth floor to keep my legs in trim. I have not used the elevator once since I have been at the hotel.'

This Gary told me with typical enthusiasm. Shortly after I took my leave... trotting down the stairs and scorning the elevator. As I made my way from the luxury of the Savoy, two thoughts flitted through my mind. In an old address book I'd looked up was the entry: Gary Player, c/o Mrs. Pither, 'Adowa,' Chobham Road, Sunningdale. That entry was 10 years old. I wonder if Gary remembers those modest lodgings, so handily placed for the nursery slopes of Wentworth and Sunningdale. Certainly he has progressed a long way since he won the 1956 Dunlop 90-hole tournament as a 20-year-old prodigy. Then I passed the ground-floor entrance to the lift, and smiled to myself, 'Gary Player needs no elevator to climb to the top.'

3

Peter Alliss

'I FEEL I'd have an even chance of beating Arnold Palmer in a series of matches but I can't say the same about taking him on in a tournament. I don't go to a tournament thinking I am going to win. Could win, yes. Will win, no. I am satisfied that this is not a matter of technique. My swing has been settled for many years, since I won the Spanish Open in 1956.

'It is a mental barrier that I have to overcome. I can't tell you if I am close to a breakthrough. The barrier is not that clearly defined. There are several things I am battling against.

'Probably the most important is that I can build up no burning desire to win at all costs. It does not bother me who wins. I just do not understand the fellows who get all burned up inside if they fail to win. I do get more keyed up in the Ryder Cup and Canada Cup. This, perhaps, is for some deep-down romantic reason. Not letting the side down, doing my bit for the old country, that kind of thing. I cannot get the same feeling when playing for myself. I cannot find the ambition to want to make thousands and thousands of pounds.

'Then, I often feel that people expect too much of me, not simply strangers in the galleries, but certain sections of the golfing Press. This is a pressure other British players don't have to bear. And there's my demeanour on the course. I try to display an air of silent, stoical calm. The result is that I sense half the watchers saying, "He's so casual, he never gets nervous, he can't be trying". And the rest say, "Miserable so-and-so, doesn't want to know you. He'd do better if he cheered up a bit". What they don't know is that if the shot, the hole or the round matters a damn your guts are churning over all the time, and you'd feel more comfortable in a small boat out in the Channel in a half-gale.'

This was Peter Alliss face to face. The heart of a top-rank golfer. Inside Alliss. The words flowed freely, chasing thoughts that sped even faster. Alliss is nothing if not articulate, perhaps the most lucid golfer I have met in more than a decade on the international tournament trail.

We arranged a pre-season encounter at Parkstone in Dorset, hard by the pines and chines and pensioned prosperity of Bournemouth, dowager duchess of water places on the South Coast. Here Peter Alliss enjoys a small kingdom of his own, among close supporters who have known him since he turned professional when 15, and, as assistant to his famous father, Percy Alliss of Ferndown, was natural heir to an illustrious golfing career.

He is close to his family, his friends and among folk who know Peter better, understand better than those of the wider world of golf, the pressures, problems, the barriers, obstacles that make up the complex lot of Peter Alliss the tournament star. Here he delights in being at the call of Parkstone members whom he serves. We met at the professional's shop, then whipped along to Alliss's imposing detached house, with impressive drive-in, two cars in the garage and a friendly greeting from a black spaniel, and a more hazardous one from a 200 lb. Pyrennean mountain dog, a magnificent St. Bernard-size animal known in Alliss circles as 'The Polar Bear'. Peter shepherded the big fellow away and explained: 'Not absolutely sure of him with strangers. He devours two pounds of meat a day. I reckon on 45$s.$ a week to keep my dogs.' A large china cabinet packed imposingly with golfing trophies engaged my attention until Peter's wife Joan joined us to sip drinks from crystal glasses. Joan left to cope with her exuberant small daughter Carol. Son Gary was at school. Lunch at a local hotel inevitably was punctuated by greetings from Peter's many friends and acquaintances.

This, then, is the setting in which Peter Alliss re-charges batteries for the rigours of the golf season ahead. It must be taken into account in any assessment of Alliss's career after more than 10 years at the top, years which in 1953 saw him make the Ryder Cup team at the age of 22, following a great third place in the Irish Open championship behind Eric Brown and Harry Weetman. The graph continued upwards with his first British tournament win in 1954, the Daks at Little Aston, and the first of nine Canada Cup appearances for England. He took the 90-hole Dunlop tournament at Wentworth in 1955 and the golf world appeared to be at Peter's feet. But then came a down period. The shadow of an unhappy début against America two years earlier cost him a place in the 1955 Ryder Cup side—his friend and contemporary Bernard Hunt receiving parallel treatment.

Not until the back end of 1956 was the Alliss star shining again. Then a 'new' Peter won the Spanish Open from a field of 10 experienced American tournament players besides a squad of British Ryder Cup men. This was the first look at the controlled, compact Alliss swing, left heel barely leaving the ground, and all temptation to hit flat out resisted. It gave Peter the 1957 P.G.A. title and a place in the historic winning Ryder Cup side at Lindrick.

The 1958 season was not a notable one for Peter in home tournaments but he made magnificent amends by winning three Continental titles in the space of 17 days in the autumn—the Italian and Spanish each by no fewer than 10 strokes, and then the Portuguese. Alliss added to his tournament wins at home with the Dunlop in 1959—a good hanging-on effort, this, at Royal Lytham—and a tie for the Sprite in 1960. Peter made another foray abroad late in 1961 to capture the Brazilian Open. He won the Schweppes P.G.A. title again at Little Aston in 1962 and 1965 at Prince's and no season goes by without at least one major tournament victory. Added to this is a record in foursomes events that speaks volumes for his disposition and tolerance as a playing partner.

This survey would not be complete without mention of an unfruitful record of only one semi-final appearance in the News of the World Match Play championship, a title won twice by Peter's father who reached the semi-final of the event five times in all. Inevitably came the comparison and the stigma that the younger Alliss was possessed of a match-play jinx, just had not the stomach for it. This canard was not laid until the 1959 Ryder Cup, where I saw Peter win his foursome with Christy O'Connor against Doug Ford and Art Wall, and in the singles refuse to die against Jay Hebert. The match was halved after Hebert had been two up with four to play. The 1961 Ryder Cup—now 18-hole matches—saw Alliss collect two and a half points, the half in his epic duel with Arnold Palmer.

At Atlanta in 1963 he went one better and defeated Palmer on American soil, and halved with the late Tony Lema. His finest hour of all came at Birkdale in the 1965 match. He won five points out of six, and his two singles victories were over U.S. Open Champions Billy Casper and Ken Venturi. But Peter has still to finish higher than eighth in the Open Championship, underlining the fact that he can summon more steel and more desire to win when playing for his country than when playing for Peter Alliss.

An imposing record? Of course. Any other golfer in the land but the gifted son of Percy Alliss would give his eye teeth to possess it. Materially successful? Yes again. Peter's solid possessions in the county of Dorset say so. Alliss's features smile at us out of the adverts, his voice is heard on radio and TV, articles flow from him, his first book has been published. He has served on the inner councils of the P.G.A. and is already a past captain of the association. A year or so back he attained one of the dreams of every golf professional . . . his autographed clubs were put on the market, with all the profit and prestige that accrue.

But to an extraordinarily large number of people Alliss's achievements are not enough. This is especially so in the sphere of tournament golf. So many, as I have recorded earlier, expect far more from him. To blame for these great expectations is, as I see it, first and foremost his pedigree: he has always had to live with people who tell him: 'I knew your famous father.'

Other factors which have led to so much being expected of Peter are the promise of his teens, his model swing, high intelligence, the brilliance of many of his performances, and almost as much as anything else his fine presence and bearing as the symbol of the British international tournament star. It is a form of hero-worship, I suppose. Some who practise it are professional observers. They would do Alliss a service to show more restraint in their partisanship.

Alliss, amplifying the pressures expounded earlier, says: 'The ones who expect so much turn and say "He's just a big bag of wind" when I don't achieve exactly what they think I should.' With indignation he added: 'What right have they to think this? Things are not happening to them—only to me. And as far as I'm concerned it is not the end of the world if I don't win every time I start.'

Reverting to his apparent poker-faced calm during tournaments, Peter said: 'Perhaps I'm all wrong. Maybe it would be better to get it out, to show my feelings. Not to throw clubs, but to express myself and not throttle my emotions. If I had my time over again I'd try it this way. My ideal would be to have a state of mind so that all tournaments were just like exhibitions, carefree, lighthearted and gay. But with my temperament I can't be like this, there is a sharp division between exhibitions and the real thing.'

Lunching with Peter Alliss is not simply a matter of roast beef and two 'wedge.' In fact the difficulty was to channel his mind to his tournament problems. The subjects ranged far and wide from the affairs of the P.G.A. to the British attitude to sport as a whole. Peter answered an attack on British professionals by Arnold Palmer. 'Where are the practice facilities, where is the weather, where is the cash for British golfers to work at the game as they do in other countries? It is all related to the traditional British outlook on world sport. Where else but here would an Olympic walking champion like Don Thompson train in a steamy bathroom to simulate conditions he would encounter abroad? Where else would a world-class diver like Brian Phelps have to go 200 miles from London—the capital, mark you—to Cardiff in order to find a suitable training pool?'

For more than two years now Alliss has thrown himself into the administrative side of the P.G.A., an interest which began during talks by the touring 1959 Ryder Cup team which were aimed at tournament reform. Alliss, John Jacobs, Bernard Hunt and Harry Weetman, in fact, stepped in where their predecessors had abdicated and inherited a decaying blueprint for tournament golf in this country.

These years of close contact with management of P.G.A. matters left Peter feeling a little bitter. 'I entered P.G.A. activities because of pride in the association. That is why I put so much thought and effort into it. The P.G.A. is not strong as a union. I wanted to make it so. What we tournament players did was in spite of what others thought. We had to retrieve what had been neglected in the past. I was extremely proud to be captain. But what did all our forward thinking and efforts to improve get us? Nothing but a feeling of distrust. Too many professionals thought we were working for our own ends. They could not believe that we were working for the good of the greatest number.

'We in turn were too trusting. The wheels were put into reverse when we were away at tournaments. I am very unhappy about one Annual General Meeting of the P.G.A. The work of a special committee on the reform of executive committee was put aside after less than 12 months' trial. There were not many more than a hundred members of the association at the meeting, which means that this small percentage runs the affairs of the association. Lack of interest coupled with lack of trust does not give one great encouragement to persist in one's efforts.'

With particular emphasis Peter concluded: 'I would like you to print this.... My interest in helping to run the P.G.A. stems from a sense of duty but I don't know how much longer I shall remain interested.'

Peter shortly after resigned from the P.G.A. Committee.

The talk seesawed back to technical matters. I suggested that Peter's performance at Palm Desert in 1959 should have ended any complexes he had about match play. He agreed and said: 'But I have still to prove myself in the match-play championship. I always seem to make people play above themselves.'

We passed on to Peter's fine record overseas, which matches if it does not surpass that at home. He said: 'Here in Britain I find myself thinking of affairs of the moment as I am about to play a shot. Once I'm away my mind is uncluttered. And I just get on with it. Here I sense what the galleries are saying and thinking and am most sensitive to it. Abroad I don't understand the caddies and I don't know the people, so nothing bothers me.'

Peter recalled the early criticisms of his qualities as a tournament golfer. 'It was freely said and written that I was a bad judge of distance. This just wasn't true. Ask any of the chaps I play with. I can club them better than I club myself. What I misjudged was the speed of my hand action, that's what caused me to knock them over the green. I always judged distance well, but way back lacked the courage to back my own assessments.

'As for the short game I never had any worries about chipping and bunker play. Putting was different. I can't help thinking of the 1954 Open when I am talking about putting. I could have won that—if I had not missed 16 or 17 putts of under five feet.'

No picture of Alliss would be complete without a corner to record his sharp and sophisticated sense of humour which, allied to an ear for authentic dialogue and his gifts as a mimic, make him such good value as a raconteur. We were discussing the surge of success that gave Peter his three Continental titles in 1958. I recalled that Joan had a part in this triumph by urging him to go out there and show 'em. Cracked Peter: 'What I didn't tell you was that we were practically broke at the time.' No quip or story from Peter will live longer than his tribute to Dai Rees on the Dunlop presentation platform after ageless Dai had won the Masters at the age of 49. Alliss said, 'Dai played my father for 20 years, he has given me a lot of trouble for another 20, and now my small son Gary is not sleeping so well at night.'

What of the future? Peter says frankly: 'Having my own clubs marketed by Slazenger's could make a big difference to me. In the past I have been just a hired hand with Ben Hogan and Gary Player the big names in the outfit. Now it is different. I feel part of it. I have a pretty lively mind and enjoy sitting in on meetings to discuss the design and marketing of Peter Alliss golf clubs. I feel I am working for one of the biggest sports equipment organisations in the world and have a duty not to let them down. The Alliss image is being pushed forward. It gives me a sense of responsibility. I have never shirked that. There is an additional sense of security. Having your name on a golf club means an ensured income for life. Just how much it means depends upon the success of the player and the firm. I would say that Bobby Locke knocked a hole in £100,000 in royalties since the war.'

Never has a tournament professional spoken more frankly of the pressures and problems affecting the man at the top. Such candour increases my admiration for the man so many people expected to be Britain's greatest golfer since Cotton. Perhaps Alliss's revelations may lead to a better understanding of him. If so, then I am certain it will help this sensitive and extremely human person.

4
Hugh Boyle

As a schoolboy Hugh Boyle went into the golf business because he found there was more money in it than distributing newspapers. At the time this was short-term planning in the Hugh Boyle scheme of things. Now, after more than a decade of work, hope and endeavour, it seems to be working out as good long-term planning as well. From the age of 15 until he was 30 Hugh worked as a willing and cheerful itinerant assistant professional with a smiling, ruddy-complexioned face, a cheery happy-go-lucky nature, and a have-clubs-will-travel attitude. He seemed to be getting nowhere but into the good graces of a wide circle of friends; he eked a precarious living from his chosen career; his latent dreams of tournament fame met only with frustration.

Then suddenly things began to happen. So fast that in the 12 months ended July 31st, 1966, Hugh's chosen tools of trade put around £4,000 tournament winnings into a hitherto thin wallet. The rain-battered 1965 Senior Service show began it. Round one was switched to the wee West Course and Boyle jumped into the lead with Wigan's Tony Coop when they both equalled Tom Haliburton's British record round of 61.

In the next stage of the tournament, foreshortened to three rounds and two days' play, Hugh led the international field by a staggering six strokes—Britain's Ryder Cup team, 10 experienced Americans, and players of a dozen other nations were behind him.

He didn't win in the end because of a ferocious last nine of 32 by the king of four-figure cheque collectors, Christy O'Connor. Hugh settled for second place with Jackie Cupit, the American who tied the 1963 U.S. Open with eventual winner Julius Boros and Arnold Palmer. With this went the reward of £1,145, a veritable fortune to the then struggling Boyle.

Hugh clutched at this first sweet taste of success with both long, strong arms. He has since proved that Dalmahoy 1965 was no two-day flash by becoming the first British Isles golfer to win a major event on the Far East circuit—the Yomiuri Open on the 1966 Canada Cup course near Tokyo—and in early June joining the select band to have won over Wentworth's legendary West Course, with the £1,000 Daks cheque as his prize.

This, then, is the late, but quick burst to fame and reasonable fortune of the lad who listened to the school pal who told him there was far more pocket money for a 13-year-old in week-end caddying at Birmingham's select Moseley club than in a newspaper round among the residents of the city district of Sparkhill, where the large and happy Irish family of Boyles grew up.

It was necessity that drove the boy Hugh to earn while still at school. There was little to spare in the kitty of a family of six children, largely dependent on father's wages as a boilerman. For two of his elder brothers were furthering their education at university and at college, one to become a priest, the other an engineer. Two other brothers have since made a successful way in life, one as circulation representative of a national newspaper, the other as a salesman. There is a sister, too, and Hugh is fifth in the family which came from Omeath, his birthplace in Co. Louth. He was brought over to Birmingham at the age of two, and apart from evacuee war years has spent all the rest of his life based in England.

Caddying hooked one more recruit to golf in Hugh Boyle, and when the time came for him to leave his Jesuit school at the age of 15, the only job he thought about doing was working as an assistant professional. It was not a living the family knew much about, which perhaps was just as well for Hugh's intentions. There were parental objections to overcome before he was allowed to start work with Bill Hennessey at Edgbaston at 25*s*. a week, £1 of which went straight to Mother.

Says Hugh: 'I got friendly with the pro at Moseley, John Morris, and when I wanted a job he sent me along to Edgbaston. After a year there I moved to Olton, another Birmingham club, under Tom Collinge, a very fine chap who is a friend to this day. After about three and a half years I moved south to Berkshire with Allan Dailey. From there I spent two winters as a teaching pro at Royal Hong Kong, following the steps of Brian Huggett out there. One summer I was attached to Coombe Wood with my friend Drew Paton. Then, in September 1961 Mr. Richard Burton invited me to join his staff at Coombe Hill. I stayed there until after the second of two winters teaching in Pakistan. I was unattached at the start of 1965 after my return from Pakistan because Mr. Burton had had to replace me with another assistant in the winter.'

These were the lean years. Fourteen of them. The years so many starry-eyed young assistants struggle through, but from which only a few break free to real achievements. If you don't think it is a hard life, then you have not heard enough stories like that of Hugh Boyle.

An underlying tenacity, a sunny, optimistic nature, and complete dedication to competitive golf got him through. This was revealed as he talked about those early years and the thoughts that filled his mind at the time.

Was he resigned to being a good club pro, which his rich and varied experience would well suit him for, or were there always tournament ambitions?

Hugh, born in Ireland on January 28th, 1936, and brought up in Birmingham, reveals neither of these backgrounds in his clear, quick, indefinable accent. He answered: 'My idea was always to try to become a good player—even if only for the reason that a bit of playing reputation helps to get a good job. Not being married I did not mind being skint so long as I could go and play in a few tournaments. As long as I kept batting I felt I was getting a little bit better, though this may have been noticeable only to myself.

'Why did it take a long time before I did anything? Lack of money had a lot to do with it . . . or the lack of confidence because of the lack of money. You did it the hard way. Obviously you could not afford a caddie all the time; you stayed and travelled cheaply; things like that. Probably it was a desperate struggle to keep going to tournaments. I was at the best clubs, but the best one could say is that it was only an existence. About £5 a week wages and half what you made from playing with members came to £6–£7 a week, that's all. The only thing was that it was good for your golf, playing all the time. You had to do this if you wanted to become a good player. So you had to stick it out. Perhaps it was a struggle, but no more so than for hundreds of lads who are doing the same right now.'

Hugh came to the tournaments, was seen around regularly at the assistants' nurseries of Coombe Hill and Hartsbourne, made forays into the big ones until the money ran out. But his achievements were small. He was just another trier.

In the Midlands he had to play second fiddle to his slightly older and more successful contemporaries Peter

Butler and Ralph Moffitt. In one of the last Youths' championship open to both professionals and amateurs he finished second.

In the big events Hugh had had a good week if he finished 29th or 41st and the £20 or £30 he took home carried him on to the next tournament.

This went on for a dozen years or more, the summer play financed in the later period by his winter teaching in Hong Kong and Pakistan. Every summer would be a season of hope . . . that the breakthrough was coming. Hugh played it alone. The current crop of golfing fairy godfathers had not arrived. He had no sponsors, benefactors, lists at the club. He is probably all the better for this.

'I did not have a thing in the sponsors line. The first real encouragement I got was from Mr. Burton. He was the first of the pros to offer a hand. Some in this country are not quite so forward. Apart from verbal advice, Mr. Burton would always be ready to go out and watch you hit balls. He was very, very good.

'He made it plain that if I was ever short of money to go to the next tournament I could always depend on him for a loan. I never had to do it—but it was a nice feeling. He has been the same to all his assistants at Coombe Hill. You don't go there unless Mr. Burton sees you are a reasonably good player. Then you learn the tournament attitude from him. He puts the final polish on your game. He was always giving you the incentive to go on trying by saying you had to be patient and go through the mill... "You must have faith and belief in yourself", was what he told us all. Being at Coombe Hill with Ken Bousfield, Neil Coles, and Tony Grubb was a big help too. It meant you were playing with better players all the time and had the opportunity to watch them.'

Hugh likes to think of his swing as unfrilled and orthodox. As with many big men, his backswing looks no more than three-quarter and well under control. He says: 'My basic swing has not changed a lot over the years. One has problems all the time. We have to work at it, you know. You don't just turn it on like a tap, or let in the clutch. The professional is constantly working on and tuning his swing. This is something the club golfer does not really grasp. They simply don't put the work into their swing that the professional can. The amateur just has not got the time.

'I have probably hit the ball reasonably well for years, but my short game was never very good. It improved a lot at Coombe Hill through Mr. Burton's advice and watching him and Ken Bousfield. My pitching improved a lot there. It was a question of being slower, more rhythmic, like Ken Bousfield, instead of giving it a good nudge.

'I don't owe my basic swing to anyone in particular. It is a gradual accumulation. I'm not exceptionally strong; length—good average, up to Neil Coles and Tony Grubb. When I'm middling the ball I'm above average, I'd say. After coming back from Pakistan in 1965 I shortened my backswing to obtain more control. I haven't any special fancies about clubs. You get used to them and stick to them; like the driver I've now had for five years; it's American—stiff shaft, light weight. I think light clubs are definitely in these days. I feel you can get more clubhead speed from the light clubs—yes, even a big fellow like me.' (Hugh is 6ft., 185 lb.).

This, then, is a summary of the background years, the years of preparation, the long apprenticeship. Another facet of Hugh's golfing education was the two winters in Pakistan. He went out for the first time when John Jacobs had to recommend a successor after his own winter coaching stints there. It happened through a chance encounter with Peter Alliss as they shared a car to Belfast

Airport from the Hennessey tournament at Clandeboye. Peter mentioned that John was looking for someone to suggest to Pakistan's arch-enthusiast Air Marshal Askar Khan. Hugh was interested and took the engagement.

'Wintering in Pakistan helped a lot, particularly in 1964–5. I was playing well when I came back then. Teaching all the time there; and one always has time to hit shots. Teaching has never clashed with tournament play for me, though I know some players find the opposite. Quite the contary, in fact. I found it made me think about the golf swing far more, especially when teaching beginners and seeing how their swings could be shaped straight away to hit the golf ball. It makes one think, "I'm making this game far too difficult."

'Teaching has cleared up a lot of things in my own mind about the swing. Grip, stance and alignment are the fundamentals for beginners. Apart from that the thing is to try to keep it as simple as you can. You wind up the body, and cock the wrists on the way up, and unwind and uncock on the way down. That is the John Jacobs principle, and I have learned a lot from John since I joined his Golf Centre early in '66. I really enjoy teaching. It is nice to see a pupil hit the ball better. It gives you a big thrill. I can always turn to teaching as a break from playing. It is never a chore.'

Now we were nearing the week Hugh found fame at Dalmahoy. I guided the conversation to his 1965 season. 'It did not begin all that well. I was failing to qualify for the last day early on. At the Silentnight, at Moortown, there was a little encouragement. I played with Roberto de Vicenzo on the last day, a wonderful fellow to play with, encourages you all the way round. I did 73, 68. The last was one of those rounds when you shoot up a lot of places and I finished 8th. I took my biggest cheque to date, £124 10s., though I had a couple of 7th places before, one of them at Moortown and the other in the 1960 Dunlop at Gleneagles, where I won my previous biggest cheque of £80.

'Then I missed qualifying in the Pringle and went on to the Open. I was second in the qualifying at Southport and Ainsdale and went on to have a good Open—my best yet. I finished joint 12th on 294, same score as Nicklaus and a stroke ahead of Palmer. There I won £182. It was only the second time I had played on the last day in five tries. I was 27th at Troon in 1962.

'The reason I was doing better? I was putting badly at the start of the season. It has always been a problem. You remember I tried putting one-handed at one time and did it right through a tournament. Last year someone told me I'd never putt collapsing the left wrist coming through the way I did.' Hugh paused to demonstrate a backhand flick with his left. 'They said you don't get an impact. The club is not accelerating; it is slowing down at impact with that action.

'So I stiffened up my action and kept the left wrist very firm through the ball. That helped tremendously on the short ones, the putts I had the most difficulty with. I began to putt very well under pressure on the short ones. From June on, I did not miss one for three or four months.'

We were now up to the Senior Service date, the last week in July. Hugh's budget did not allow for entry in the Continental championships around this time, so he went early to Edinburgh and made his customary base with his friends the Watts, near Barnton Golf Club. 'I went to Dalmahoy and practised alone, carried my own clubs, put down several balls at every hole, and was hitting it fairly well. But the reconnaisance was wasted the first day, when after it rained and rained we began the tournament on the short course as an emergency. I walked the back nine holes of the short course on the Thursday evening, being told they were the ones to look at. There was no question of anyone practising on it. Next day I trotted out there with Grant Aitken (he did 65) and had a three, three, two start, which I thought was very nice. I got it out in 30, and was 31 back, with a four at the short 15th. My thoughts? Well, I must qualify with that,' grinned Hugh.

'I slept very well that night. Next day I shot 68 in the morning. I just kept batting. It shook me to hear the announcement: ". . . and that gives Boyle the lead by six shots." My immediate reaction was, "Hello, I've often wondered how it would feel to lead the tournament by six. Boyle, you are about to find out." I did not eat much lunch.

'I was playing with Jack Cupit, the American, and gained eight shots on him in that second round. He was 63, 76 to my 61, 68. Then, as you know, he went out in 30 in the afternoon, chipping in, holing everything.

'Honestly, I can tell you now that what he was doing did not really worry me. The papers were all wrong to say that his scoring cost me the tournament. Whatever your partner is doing, your only worry is getting round the course yourself. That's my reaction, anyway. All I thought about in that afternoon round was not taking 80; not blowing; whether I would get it round or not.

'Cupit birdied 10 and made his ninth shot on me in 10 holes. But I got away from him again and in the end he caught me only at the last hole. Christy O'Connor caught me with what I reckon was a fabulous last nine holes, 32. I reckon I played well to get back in 37 for 75. I did not play badly, and my only real mistakes were to take three from the edge three times.

'Losing after having that big lead certainly has not damaged my morale. I was chuffed, delighted. I did not lose the tournament, Christy won it. All my fellow pros tell me that. I thought at lunchtime I'd win if I got it round in 76. Someone would have to do a low 60s score to beat that, and that takes some doing at Dalmahoy. Christy did, and that was it.'

Whatever the result, Hugh Boyle had his day—his 61, his six-shot lead, his first four-figure cheque. But there is an ironic footnote to the inside story of Hugh's first success story.

He was not going to play in the tournament at all. In fact, the final day, July 31st, was going to be his wedding day! Said Hugh ruefully: 'Ironic, wasn't it? The tournaments had not gone well earlier in the season. The money I had saved in Pakistan was dwindling. I was prepared to take a club job, but there wasn't one. I asked my fiancée to wait. She refused. . . . I played at Dalmahoy. I must confess I got my watch out after playing five or six holes on the Saturday morning and thought, "Hmm. Twelve o'clock. I'd just about be saying 'I do'." '

Hugh Boyle got one of the breaks his big-hearted trying deserved at the end of the 1965 season. A sponsored trip to the Far East circuit. 'I had a really lucky break,' he says. 'Tom Collinge, my old boss at Olton, asked me to do a locum job while he took a couple of weeks' holiday. It was nice going back. I still had many friends there. I was invited to a club film show one evening and there I met Mr. David Wiseman, a member and wealthy patron of sport in the Midlands—former chairman of Birmingham City, contractor, property, tremendous interest in sport. We were chatting and he asked:

' "When are you playing again?"

' "In the spring," I told him.

' "You ought to go away. I'll take care of it for you."

'I thanked him warmly and said I'd find out more about the Far East tour. I couldn't say "Yes" right away. I mean, it's the sort of thing you dream about happening. I dared not build up my hopes too much. I did write to Kim Hall in Hong Kong. It took a long time to get a reply. Then I phoned Mr. Wiseman again. He said, "You'd better come along to see me." I told him the financial details. The next thing I knew was him saying "You'd better get your air ticket", and he was writing out a cheque. There was no question of being able to pay back, share of winnings. It was a gift. You can imagine my debt to Mr. Wiseman.'

Hugh had his interview in November, flew out in February—to a fruitless first four tournaments. 'The greens out there are so different, so difficult. I never thought I could hit the ball so well and finish about 27th. But it happened on those long, spiky greens. At Hong Kong and Taipei they were better.

'When we got to Japan it was like playing at home—cool, dull, a lot of breeze on the last day... thank God. I did 68, 71, 71, 76. Led by five shots after three rounds and won by two from Teddy Ball, the Australian with whom I became great friends on the tour. Funny thing, we decided on the way out to the course that we would room together... and finished 1, 2.

'The Indian Open at Delhi was a complete contrast—scorching weather. I led after one round, was a shot behind Peter Thomson after two, and finished tying for second with Guy Wolstenholme and Major Sethi, the India amateur who won it the year before. If I could have putted I would have won.

'You could say I went to the Far East to learn and stayed to earn. But I did learn too—chiefly that if you don't putt you'll never do any good in professional golf. The greens are so much more difficult in the hot countries that you have to putt better. It is good for you to play on those greens. You must strike the ball 100 per cent or there's no chance of getting the ball in the hole. In Britain our greens are so good that an imperfectly struck putt often creeps into the hole.'

The 1966 season at home began inauspiciously for Hugh. He missed the last day in three of his first five tournaments before winning the Daks.

'My record goes up and down like a yo-yo, doesn't it?' said Hugh with his ready grin. 'It is all because of the short game. I have often played super golf without getting the putts in. I went over to the Peter Alliss putting style, left hand below right, at Long Ashton for the Martini and got on fairly well with it. I switched back for the Blaxnit, but changed again at Wentworth and did 68 in the pre-qualifying. I stuck to it then. Peter Alliss is a real convert. "Just hinge the right hand and hit", is all there is to it, he says.

'My only problems are with the short game now. I am very pleased with the way I am hitting the ball this year. John Jacobs helped me tremendously when I went over to the Leopardstown driving range in January. I did a lot of coaching over there and John gave me a check-up before I went to the Far East.

'I was standing too much to the right of the target and hooking the ball too much. He got me to stand more left, or square and strike through the ball more. This really has been a bigger help than anything else, because it has got me hitting the ball a little harder under pressure. That has made me a lot more confident. John made a slight alteration to my grip too—the right hand was probably a little too strong. He got me to keep it more on top and bring the hands closer together.'

Hugh said perhaps the most significant thing of all when putting forward the final reason for the breakthrough to the big league in that July 1965 Senior Service performance. He summed up: 'It's all in the mind. It is a matter of realising you are good enough. Doing well in the Open at Birkdale—I was joint 12th—was a beginning. It has all flowed nicely from there.'

Important milestones were passed in 1967. Hugh attained Ryder Cup rank. His continued presence in the top ten in tournaments saw to that. He went home to win the Irish championship, and a coveted place in Ireland's team of two for the World Cup tournament.

Things are rolling for Hugh Boyle now. He has the finest advice, a secure base job with the John Jacobs Golf Centres, appreciative and helpful friends, success is coming in the tournaments, his swing has stood the test of winning. But, by the shades of Ben Hogan, he has worked for it. The turn in fortune has come not before time.

5

Christy O'Connor

TALKING to Christy O'Connor about the Open championship is a serial story that reaches back to 1951. It covers the age from Hogan to Nicklaus. It saw the period of Peter Thomson dominance. It even went back to the last British win, by inimitable Max Faulkner at Royal Portrush —which is where the then unknown young man from County Galway came in.

Consider the impressive record O'Connor has built since then. As a raw and untried competitor who had never played outside his native Ireland, Christy not only qualified at Portrush but finished joint 19th in his first Open. It was an apt overture to a record that has not been matched over the last decade or so by a player from the British circuit.

Christy has played through to the last day of the Open every time he has competed. He did not come to Lytham in 1952, but from '53 on the sequence has continued unbroken. In the same period only Syd Scott, the Ryder Cup stylist from Roehampton, showed the same consistency. Scott went 13 years from 1950 to 1962 before missing the last day by one shot at Lytham in '63.

In his 16 Open championships up to 1967 O'Connor has finished in the first 10 eight times. Only twice has he been outside the first 20. Only once has he been on the limit score for qualifying for the final 36 holes—at Troon,

1962—and of this more in Christy's own words later. His performances take in eight of the classic links—St. Andrews (four times), Birkdale (three), Carnoustie (once), Hoylake (twice), Lytham (twice), Muirfield (twice) Portrush (once), and Troon (once). He was joint runner-up in 1965, has finished joint third (twice), once joint fifth, and sixth and joint sixth.

Christy's greatest bid for the most coveted crown in golf will be remembered as at Royal Lytham St. Annes in 1958. A four at the 72nd hole, instead of the one-over-par five a bunkered drive cost him, would have gained a tie with Peter Thomson, the eventual winner, and the then 23-year-old Dave Thomas.

This is not the only Open he might have won. Christy's unluckiest year came 12 months later at Muirfield where South Africa's Gary Player put his name on the hallowed pot with a storming last-day aggregate of 138. O'Connor shared fifth place four strokes off Gary's 284 total. But share Christy's reflections on that distant battle:

'Muirfield was my bravest Open. I was taken ill after nine holes of practice and I had never seen the course before. I had an abscess which was so bad that the doctors told me there was no chance of playing. I had to plead with them to do something about it. I was successful in persuading them to patch me up and I struggled to the tee and qualified. I was in such discomfort that I could not tee my ball. The caddie had to do it.'

Christy, in fact, got up from his sick-bed to shoot a 72 at Gullane on the first qualifying day and followed with a 71 the first time he ever played a full round at Muirfield. But even Christy's rugged constitution could not combat the strain of a weakening illness *and* the opening rounds of the championship. He had to settle for a start of 73, 74 behind the surprise front-runner, Fred Bullock.

On 147 Christy was only a shot inside the qualifying

score in a championship which took an unaccountable toll of the established fancies. Player was back in the pack on 146 after two rounds. On the gruelling Friday, when at that time a 36-hole inquisition separated the champion from the rest, O'Connor's 72, 69 was bettered by only one man—Player, the winner, with 70, 68.

Said Christy, still making no excuses over his fitness: 'The ninth hole cost me that championship. I had three fives and a six there.' Muirfield's long ninth, with narrow fairway, out of-bounds wall, tight bunkering and headwind took toll of many more beside Christy in the campaign of 1959.

The Open O'Connor is most remembered for took place a year before his ill-fated Muirfield venture. It happened at the course which seems fated to produce photo-finish Open championships, Royal Lytham. A four at 18 on the final round would have given O'Connor a tie with Thomson and Thomas on 278.

Scot Eric Brown and Leopoldo Ruiz, newcomer from the Argentine, stood in the same position of opportunity. Brown, bursting up from the pack with a third round 65 —in which he was home in 30, an Open record—wanted a four for 277. He took a six—bunkered drive, then a heart-breaking three putts.

The spectacular Ruiz, dubbed the longest hitter of iron shots in the world at that time, had made his challenge with a 65 in the second round. He stood on the last tee wanting a four to tie. He took a six.

O'Connor, however, was the 36-hole leader—67, 68— 135, from Ruiz 136, Thomson and Thomas 138. Thomson, 66 in the first round, made a third-round surge with 67. He led with 205, and needed to because he used 73 blows in the last round and the pack was closing fast.

Thomas was partnering Thomson and shot 69, 71 for the last day. Both bettered the 279 target set by Brown nearly an hour earlier. Then came O'Connor and Ruiz, the two leaders paired last of all and facing the massed expectant gallery which had just billowed round the last hole with Thomson and Thomas. Let Christy take up the story:

'Ah, Lytham in 1958. I was playing really well that year. I fell in love with the greens as soon as I got there. I thought the Open was mine after my satisfying start in the first two rounds. People still talk to me about the 18th hole in the last round, but I did not feel that hole lost it for me. Where I lost it was in the first nine holes in the afternoon.

'Peter Thomson and Dave Thomas were in front of us with the biggest part of the crowd. They lost a complete hole on the match in front by the ninth. I don't blame them, they are not slow players. It was the sheer numbers of people the stewards had to try to control. It made our progress very slow, and did not help my scoring.'

The same army of spectators added to the problem of the last tee shot for O'Connor and Ruiz.

Christy recalls: 'The stewards and police did their best to get the crowd back on the right of the fairway. They just could not clear it and we left with only half the fairway to play. I hit a well-struck drive with slight draw on it. The bounce was to the left and it went in the left-hand bunker. I could not make the green from the sand, put my third 20 feet from the pin and just missed the putt.'

So ended the Irish maestro's Open championship hopes for 1958.

O'Connor was to fill third place again in 1961, tied with Neil Coles on 288 behind Arnold Palmer (284), winning the first of two Opens, and Dai Rees (285), runner-up for the third time. But Christy was nothing like so close to winning as he had been three years earlier. The Thursday-morning gale which made such a shambles of the Open's tented township saw to that.

O'Connor was right there with an opening 71. Then came a gale-defying 77 which kept him just in sight of the leaders. 'That 77 was a fantastic round for the day,' O'Connor recalls.

Play on Friday was put off by a deluge. Christy says he putted like a magician in his third round of 67. It was not enough to close the gap on Palmer and Rees. The touch deserted him in his final round of 73 and he dropped a further shot to the two leaders. This can be reckoned one of O'Connor's best-played championships. He was beaten only by the presence of two superb golfers—Palmer and the gallant Rees, leading the home challenge at the age of 48.

O'Connor does not rank St. Andrews as his favourite Open championship course. This honour he divides between Portrush, Lytham, Birkdale and Muirfield. Nevertheless, he has played two good Opens at the home of golf, besides one moderate one and one rank bad one. In 1964 Christy tied with Harry Weetman for sixth place behind the late Tony Lema, and they were the most serious challengers to the dashing American at the 36-hole stage . . . Lema 141, Weetman 143, O'Connor 144.

'I always started my rounds badly at St. Andrews. I couldn't play the first five or six holes well enough. And I had a six and a five at the 17th on the last day,' sums up Christy. He finished 12 strokes behind Lema on 291.

In his first Open at St. Andrews, however, in 1955, a score of 287, though only six strokes behind winner Peter Thomson, earned only a tie for 10th place. That was the year of O'Connor's breakthrough to the ranks of big tournament winners. He did it in some style, for the first tournament he won was the first in which a £1,000 prize had been put up in Britain; the Penfold-Swallow at Southport in May '55. With his new-found confidence,

Christy steadily went 71, 75, 70 for the first three rounds of what was but his third Open.

Then he had a burst of brilliance round the Loop, of such effect that he can say: 'I did have a chance to win. I remember I was playing with John Jacobs and we reckoned on the 14th tee I could win if I did fours in. That must have been fatal—I took an eight at the 14th after hitting a perfect tee shot. I took a driver for my second, when I should have played a safe spoon shot . . . and went into Hell Bunker.' Fours in from the 14th is asking a lot, but it is not impossible at St. Andrews. One can never count on anything at the unpredictable and venomous Old Course, as even winner Thomson found in 1955, when the 14th extracted a seven from him on his last round. Peter, fortunately, had shots to spare.

The 1957 Open at St. Andrews—Bobby Locke's fourth —was a moderate one for Christy. He qualified comfortably but got off on the wrong foot with a 77 and had to burn out a 69 to make sure of playing the final 36 holes. His 291 total was good enough for only 19th place.

The Centenary Open in 1960 brought the Irish wizard's poorest championship yet—a 294 total and joint 36th place. Ireland was full of hope after their man had chased Gary Player home for the honour of leading the qualifiers. Then came a tragic reaction. O'Conner began the championship with the millstone of an 80. He pulled a fighting 67 out of the bag to stay in, but was never in contention for anything but the continuance of his record in the championship. Christy says now: 'It must have been reaction after the Canada Cup in Portmarnock only two weeks before the Open. I had been concentrating so much on that.'

It is obvious from his record that the Open has always provided a great challenge to O'Connor. One can bracket him with Dai Rees in saying he has won every other honour in the game. Christy's reaction to the two terrible starts he had in championships at St. Andrews point to the pride he takes in putting up his best possible performance in the Open. When others would have lain down to their fate and said 'It's not my year,' O'Connor buckles to and produces a sub-par round.

Like Rees, too, he has tried all tactics to win the Open. The greatest disaster and the greatest lesson came, perhaps, at Troon in 1962. Christy tells the story: 'I had never played Troon. I felt I must get to know it thoroughly. I went there 10 days before the championship started. I played it in hurricanes, in the calm, 27 and 36 holes a day. By the time the championship started I was burned out.' Christy began 74, 78 and was never in sight of Palmer and Nagle, who fought out the championship on their own.

'It was the biggest lesson I had had,' O'Connor continued. 'You must be fresh and well rested for the Open, or any other tournament you badly want to win. If you are tired you just don't think properly, and then you've no chance.' Christy's 297 on the fractious and toughly prepared Troon links was 21 strokes behind Palmer's total, but still good enough for joint 16th place.

In the 1965 Open at Birkdale, O'Connor followed his own formula of ensuring that he was mentally fresh for the championship by missing out a sponsored tournament in order to take a rest at Southport before the battle began. He arrived 10 days before the tee-off and for seven days the closest he got to any serious work was making a call on Bobby Halsall, Royal Birkdale's professional, and having a walk on the course. He relaxed on the beach, he watched the children on the miniature railway, he slept to build up a store of nervous energy.

He made the essential good start—a 69. But his finishing was not sharp enough in the middle rounds. He took 73 and 74. He came again with 71 in the final round. It earned a tie for second place, but it never put Christy in real striking distance of halting the march of Australia's Melbourne Tiger, Peter Thomson, to his fifth Open title. It ended Thomson 285, O'Connor and Brian Huggett 287.

The 'hayfields' of Muirfield in the controversial 1966 Open did not trouble the accurate O'Connor. His putting did, however, Thus, with rounds of 73, 72, 74, 72—291, he finished nine behind Jack Nicklaus to share 13th place with Harold Henning.

Christy had no record at all when he ended 19th to Faulkner at Portrush at the age of 26. But he was on the way up. In 1953 and '54 he won the Ulster championship, defeating Fred Daly in one of the match-play finals. Then he made his first impact on the big circuit at the 1954 Penfold-Swallow event. He remembers having to do a recovery 67 after 78 in the first round of the qualifying. In the ensuing match play he collected the scalps of both the top Scots, John Panton and Eric Brown. He wound up a wonderful week by having the temerity to take the regal Henry Cotton to the 23rd in their semi-final. Cotton went on to beat John Jacobs in the final.

The big breakthrough of that first £1,000 win was to follow in just a year. The 1955 season saw O'Connor firmly established as a tournament star. He went to Thunderbird with the Ryder Cup team, the first of an uninterrupted run of appearances against America. He won the Dunlop Masters in 1956, the News of the World Match Play in 1957, and in 1958 shared that unforgettable Canada Cup victory with Harry Bradshaw in Mexico City. 'That was one of my greatest thrills, Harry and I winning in Mexico. I was just as excited to be on the winning team in the Ryder Cup at Lindrick, though,' O'Connor says.

In the summer of 1959 Christy collected his second

£1,000 cheque in the Daks tournament at Wentworth, one of his happiest hunting grounds. Since then he has stepped up for four-figure prize money more than a dozen times, a record which puts him way ahead of any player on the British circuit.

What makes the farmer's son from Galway the great player he is? He is an acknowledged master of iron play. 'Irons never worry me, I never practise them much,' he says.

I remember him once telling me, though, that the way to perfect long iron shots was to practise them off sand, a method he had adopted on the shores of his native Galway. 'You have to hit them well off sand or you get no shot at all,' he said.

Christy says his swing used to be far looser and more wristy than it is now. 'I have tightened it up. This has helped me a lot. I don't hit the ball as hard now but I am a lot straighter off the tee. It is better that way. I have worked on my tee shots a lot over the years.'

Christy has won on big courses—Portmarnock, the Burma Road; and he has won on tricky little ones—Woodbrook, Longniddry. And it is his deadly short game that has won him as much money as any other department of his play.

The 'trade' says, 'When Christy is putting he can win everything.' His putting does tend to come in streaks. But his little wedge shots often take all the trouble out of putting, so accurate is he in lobbing the ball into the shadow of the pin. Christy's philosophy on this is simple: 'One thing you must realise is that you are going to miss up to five greens in a round no matter who you are. That is where power of recovery tells. I spent hours and hours and hours on the short game and putting.'

O'Connor is obviously such a good pressure player that it is puzzling to think that he has not gone even closer in the Open championship. Simply, he answers: 'This is the greatest pressure tournament of all. We are all trying too hard.'

Farmer's son Christy climbed in a comparatively short time from the obscurity of being the professional at the modest nine-hole Bundoran course in Co. Donegal into undreamed of acclaim and wealth. He has taken it well. He remains unspoiled and humble, taking defeat philosophically, and victory with dignity. The strain of tournaments has punished his health at times, but he relaxes easily between his battles. He still bears, after a dozen or so years at the top, an air of bewilderment about it all. He still takes pleasure in his acceptance by his fellow professionals. Christy goes out of his way to emphasise: 'They are a great bunch of lads on the circuit.'

You're a great lad yourself, Christy.

6

Dave Thomas

DAVE THOMAS was not winning the tournament at the time I had chosen to broach a certain question to him at one of the stops on the big-money circuit. But his demeanour could not have been more relaxed and confident if that Saturday's four-figure cheque had been folded safely in his wallet. The towering Thomas, looking as big and strong and four-square as if a sculptor had done a quick job on a huge cube of granite, was still glowing from the deep satisfaction of a tournament that had gone before.

Little Aston, 1966. This was be charted as an historic battlefield in the far from completed chronicles of Dave Thomas. He won the Penfold-Swallow tournament there—holing a 20 ft. birdie putt on the last green to do it—and so broke a barrier that had been blocking and tormenting him for one-third of his young life. The golf world was told in letters inches high that this was the then 31-year-old David's first outright stroke-play tournament success in his native country. He had waited a long 10 years for it.

He was Belgian Open champion at 20; runner-up in the Canada Cup individual championship at 23; French Open champion in 1959. More still, in 1958, still only 23, he tied for the Open championship with Peter Thomson at Royal Lytham St. Annes. He lost the play-off, but the performance remains the closest a British golfer has been to winning the Open since Max Faulkner was successful in 1951.

But eight years were to pass before Dave was to win his first major stroke event in Britain. In between came the consolation of the News of the World Match Play championship (1963), two Esso Round Robin victories, Ryder Cup rank, stroke-play victories abroad—perhaps the greatest of these to head the U.S. Open qualifying competition in 1964—and a tie with Ireland's Jimmy Martin for the Silentnight at Moortown in 1965. As the Scots caddie observed upon another occasion, 'It's no' possible, but it's a fact'. This seems the only possible comment on the incredible gap in Dave's magnificent record.

I gave the satisfying impact of that Little Aston victory time to sink in before asking Thomas what it meant to him. It was a good question. Dave is one of the most rewarding of Britain's leading players to talk to. He is uncomplicated. He is candid. He is frank and honest. And extremely lucid when he gets going.

That victory to Thomas was many things. A release. Fulfilment. The salve to an open wound. The retort to a thousand critics. Almost certainly the platform for further success.

'Winning at Little Aston does mean a tremendous amount. I feel less tense. My record is sort of complete now. I don't have to rush any more now that I have won this first medal tournament. Previously everything I played in had this barrier hanging over it—it could be the first one, the one I have been waiting for. So I've always felt I had to rush. Now it is different. I've won match play, I've won medal, I've won several European championships, two tournaments in New Zealand. I have won everything I have to win to prove I am a top-class golfer.

'I suppose being second in the Canada Cup and tieing
E

for the Open championship makes me a little bit better than most and this is what I feel now. So no one can come up to me and say "That was a bad shot" or "That was a bad chip" or "That was a bad putt". I can turn round and tell them to buzz off, that they don't know what they are talking about.

'These are my thoughts now, whereas before I felt frustrated—yes, frustrated, that is the word,' continued Dave. 'I felt I should have won so much, so many, so long before... and never quite done it.'

Heavens! How he must have been frustrated. To have tied for the Open, to be unchallengeably the best driver in the British Isles for the last 10 years, to putt with the best of them, to be a good finisher—as best proven in the 1959 French Open—and to possess such a record in match play... all these qualities must have made it intolerable for Dave to live with the thing that must have seemed as elusive and intangible as the crock of gold at the end of a rainbow. But live with it he had to, and probably worse, he knew why he had to.

It was all because of his chipping. It was the giant's Achilles heel, the chink in Dave's armour. The soft little shot 10 to 20 yards from the flag over lush grass, a bunker or a bank has plagued Thomas's golfing life, threatened it with ruin. He has done everything to eliminate the weakness. Everyone in golf has advised him. He has worked at it like a slave. But no. The fault persisted. The legend grew, until it passed into the fabric of golfing lore with Max Faulkner's gay dressing, Bobby Locke's hook, Peter Thomson's sang-froid, Arthur Lees's cuppy lies, Peter Alliss's Ryder Cup début, Dai Rees's chattering, and the latent drama of Arnold Palmer.

I apologise to Dave for bringing it up, for the legend is on the way out. And nothing has done more harm in perpetuating it than the constant and too often snide reference to Thomas's unfortunate difficulty. It is on the way out because Dave does not let it worry him any more. He has grown to live with it. And as a result he has less trouble with it. The bad chip doesn't crop up so often. Mentally and technically he is on the way to mastering it. If he had not there would have been no Penfold-Swallow victory, no tie with Jimmy Martin in the Silentnight. No gallant runner-up effort in Jack Nicklaus's Open at Muirfield.

The barricade has not suddenly fallen to Thomas. But gradually over the past two seasons he has begun to master the chip. How and why is quite a story. I will let Dave tell it from the beginning.

'It is a difficult shot for anyone—even Bernard Hunt, Peter Alliss and Harry Weetman miss them. Harry, a particularly good chipper, with a tremendous touch around the greens, tells me there are times when he has difficulty. On a particular course or particular occasion the thought does enter their heads that they can miss this sort of shot. But more often than not they get away with it. They might not hit it 100 per cent, but they get away with it. They do so because they can keep their rhythm going.

'This is the thing I find difficult—to keep the rhythm going. I can make an attempt at it, but because I'm sort of holding on to it, jerking it, getting tense over it, there's no chance of the rhythm being there. This is the thing that sends the ball 10 yards through the green or not on the green at all. If you can keep the rhythm going, even if you top it the ball is still going to finish somewhere round about, and you get away with a bad one. I've never been able to get away with a bad one because of lack of rhythm, because of this tenseness. Now I am making more of an attempt to keep the rhythm going, so that I hit it smoothly, instead of a quick "let's get it over" jerk.

'It's not that I can't use a wedge. Give me a full shot

and I'm perfectly happy. The very short shots around the green have been the difficult ones. Because I'm so big and strong I don't have to take the club back more than two feet and I can hit 100 yards. You must have seen me hit the ball into some peculiar places from such a short shot. The fear of these uncontrolled shots has transferred itself, sort of built up so that I was incapable of releasing the club smoothly. It became that quick jab which could do all sorts . . . over the green, into the trap in front of me, knock the ball anywhere.

'No, the lack of rhythm on this shot does not affect or apply to any other shot at all. I'm a good putter. And that's rhythm. It's exactly the same thing. Unless you've got rhythm in your putting you can't possibly lag up a long putt. The least jerk and you lose control of distance, the least tenseness and you jerk. Then it goes that extra two feet past and you miss the next. This is something I've always known. I wasn't taught. It's feel. There's no way of measuring a long putt, no choice of club, you can't measure how far you take the club back. It's feel and rhythm, not giving it a jerk.

'I have not in the past been able to transfer this feel to a chip. I get "that" '—Dave demonstrated a nervous, quick convulsive jab—'at the last second. It is anxiety, the fear of a bad result. I must say in the last 18 months I have been getting better and better. I still miss the occasional one, but everybody does. Bill Large missed one in the recent Martini, but it didn't stop him tieing. I don't suppose he'll get stuck with it for life. But when I first began missing one, and then missed another the following week as well, people began to say "Oh, Dave Thomas can't chip". It built up and built up, until suddenly I realised myself that Dave Thomas can't chip. It got worse from then on. As soon as I realised I was not very good at chipping, then I was not very good at chipping. It began to get on top of me about 1960. It was there in 1958 or earlier, but it never got me down because I was so good at other parts of the game. I thought, "This is going to come." But it didn't come. I got all this comment and publicity, people saying and writing, "He's not very good there," —and I got worse.

'As you know, everybody tried to help me ... Walter Burkemo, Tony Cerda, Angelini and Grappasonni in Italy, Norman von Nida, Bernard Hunt, Peter Alliss and John Jacobs, Gerald Micklem and Raymond Oppenheimer. Each year you think this is going to be the year you've mastered it. You practise in the winter and you get it going reasonably well. Then you play in the first tournament and you get a chip. You give it a jerk ... and you're back where you started last year.'

'Has it been this shot alone that held you back all those years?'

'No question of that, no question at all,' was Dave's answer to my brief prompting of his flow of thought. 'It puts so much pressure on the rest of your game. Unbelievable pressure. You feel you've got to hit every green, devise shots that will avoid having to play the orthodox chip. Even though my long game stood up to it I knew there had to be a time when it wouldn't. It doesn't even have to come apart ... you hit the side of a green and it jumps off instead of on ... and you've got a chip, you've suddenly got what you've been trying to avoid. You go round after round after round without one, but you're expecting it, waiting for it, dreading it.

'Now I'm thinking differently. I feel it will come, but I am ready for it. I'm going to get one; so what? That's how I feel now. If I three-putted the next green—which I probably won't—it will cost a shot just the same. I am not afraid of three-putts, everybody three-putts. So you accept three-putts as a misjudgment. I am now prepared to accept a chip as a misjudgment and get on with the next shot.'

'Did this attitude just grow, or was there anything that helped you to get it?'

Promptly Dave replied: 'Oh, yes, moving to Dunham. Without question. Taking a club job at the beginning of 1965 has had a profound affect. The fact that it was Dunham Forest is more important still.

'At the end of 1964 I had just a year to go of my five-year contract with Dunlop which enabled me to be a playing professional at Sunningdale. In each of the past four years I found it becoming harder and harder to rely on my golf with a wife, growing family, house, mortgage, and the whole lot. I had a lot to make before I broke even. I did well enough, winning £2,500 to £3,000 in each of those years. But it was becoming harder and harder. Long iron shots and drives which were just automatic weren't any more. I'd come off them a little bit and not hit them as well as I used to.

'So I decided that with only one year of the contract to go I must start looking for a job. What really clinched it was that unfortunate experience I had in the match play [Walton Heath, 1964] when as defending champion I was asked to qualify when 12 other players were exempt because they were going to the Carling in America. This stuck a little bit, even though I tried to pass it off by thinking, "Well, there's the chance of an extra £200 if I win the qualifying," I still thought it was wrong for the holder to qualify. [The match play champion has since been exempted from qualifying.]

'Also, you'll remember, Robbie and the kids had been in Australia for six months while I had been playing in America. They were due at Southampton that day, the second day of the qualifying. That was in my mind as well: the thought of seeing them all again. I went out a bit on edge and didn't play very well—and when I missed a short putt for a six on the 14th I smashed the ball off the green. I could have holed out in seven and still qualified with par for the last four holes. But that was it. I banged the ball away as it went by the hole. That was just a release. I felt better after that. But I felt that I just had to get a job. I felt I had to get away. I didn't want to see the tournaments. I almost went to The Hague. And that was how I went to Dunham.

'Archie Preston [captain of Dunham Forest] came to see me at Sunningdale and asked me to go and have a look at it. All I knew about Dunham was that it was Alex Hay's club. I looked it up in the *Golfers' Handbook*, and thought, "I can't see myself moving to Manchester for a nine-hole course". Still, I motored there one morning, drove into the car park, walked round the clubhouse...and I knew this was *it*, just as straight away as that. I met the committee and it was just a question of when I could start. There was no doubt in my mind. They looked as if they were trying to do something that I felt should be done in this country, building a golf and country club with everything done on luxury lines. They weren't afraid to charge the members for it, and if you couldn't afford it, well, you just weren't a member. This is what golf is like all round the world except the British Isles and I think it has got to come in this country. To have gone to a club with a wooden hut as the pro's shop would have buried me. In fact, I don't think I would have stayed in this country at all.

'But at Dunham everything is done right and properly and I feel very much at home. I am contented, I have roots, Robbie and I can see the next 10 years mapped out for us: where the kids are going to school, everything like that. Robbie doesn't like the Manchester climate, but then it rains everywhere. Then, of course, I've got

Fred Bullock as a teaching professional. We have the perfect set-up. The club has the best of both worlds, a first-class teacher and a tournament professional.'

What of the way ahead? With a secure base, life well organised, how does Dave feel about his playing future?

'I feel I can do better, because, as I've said, there's not this chase any more. I think it just a question of waiting for the right circumstances, the right course, the right time, then I can win anything. But it has to be a good golf course. The better the course, the happier I feel. Put me on a fiddling course, then I hate it. It's foreign to me to fiddle it, and bounce it, and jump it around. I can't play that kind of golf.

'It is not length alone. Little Aston was little over 6,500 yards and there were one or two shortish chip holes. It is more the shape of the course, the shape of the holes. Turnberry is my kind of course, Moor Park when it is soft, but not when it is hard. I don't mind seaside courses where you have to bounce, because they lend themselves to bouncing. You can work the ball, there is more space, close turf on which you can play a pitch and run or putt from off the green. I find it hard to pitch over long grass and open ground. Sometimes when I've got a bunker in front of me I'll play a better pitch than when there's no other shot. It's got to be pitched over the bunker. If there is a clear fairway I'm thinking whether I should run it, or chip it, or putt it. That indecision is often fatal.'

We were back on 'that' subject again and Dave was saying, 'I'm sick and tired of people forever criticising this one shot instead of just forgetting it or accepting it. This is what I am doing now, accepting it. If I see Bernard Hunt hook a drive, I accept it—O.K., so Bernard hooked a drive.

'Every successful player has his weakness. Peter Alliss and his short putts—he has tried everything. Bernard

Bernard Hunt (Hartsbourne Country Club). Plundered the British tournament circuit during 'Golden Year' of 1963

Christy O'Connor (Royal Dublin). No player in the British Isles matches the consistency of the Irish ace in the Open

Dave Thomas (Dunham Forest). Golfing giant who wrestled with and finally defeated the jinx which threatened his career

Jimmy Hitchcock (Croydon Driving Range). 1960 Master Golfer. His creed, 'A quitter never wins a winner never quits'

Michael Bonallack (Thorpe Hall). Amateur champion many times over; captain of British and English international teams

Hugh Boyle (John Jacobs Golf Centres). Irish champion, 1967.
It took fifteen years' hard trying before he got to the top

Hunt can't drive through a gap—he'll take a three-wood and leave it short. I think nearly everyone who plays has got something he doesn't like. But a lot of them won't admit it. They must have something, or they'd win everything. Look at Christy O'Connor, he is probably the worst putter for such a tremendous player with a tremendous record. The rest of his game is there all the time. There isn't a shot he can't play. When he has a putting streak no one can touch him, and he still wins when he is putting moderately.'

Dave Thomas talks so much sense that you wonder why it has taken so long to sort out his own problems. But there's no truer saying than 'learning the hard way'. Dave certainly has. The mental punishment he must have taken since he tied for the 1958 Open would be enough to send most people if not to digging ditches, then the security of a quiet club job. Propped by his massive talent, Dave has battled on with an obstinate kind of courage that is typical of the British. History tells us that this quality often wins the last battle. Here's hoping it does for Dave Thomas.

7

Michael Bonallack

MICHAEL BONALLACK was not long back from his first appearance in the U.S. Masters tournament when we talked about life at the top in amateur golf, the years which bridged his first Amateur championship, at Turnberry in 1961, and his second victory in the blue riband event, at Porthcawl in 1965. Perhaps the most striking thought he expressed was in this one sentence, 'Every time I go to America I think I learn something.'

There, I thought, is the essence of this golfer's greatness. Such humility towards the stern and exacting game of golf was a revealing aspect of the player who bestrides the amateur tournament scene in Britain like a colossus.

It was, and at the same time it wasn't the sort of thing you would expect to hear from the man who had done everything in the field of amateur golf by the time he was 30 years old. It was not the utterance, one would think, of the superman golfer, the dominant competitor who had gone from success to success over the past five seasons, winning a major national title in each one of them. Would one expect it of the man who has rewritten the records books to the tune of being the first ever to take the British and English Amateur titles in one season; the first to win the English Amateur championship four times; with a record number of international appearances for England,

and been captain of his country more times than anyone else?

But he did say it, and it is this very modesty and willingness to learn that makes Michael the golfer he is. It is not the first time I have observed a humbleness towards the demands of the game as the key quality in a great golfer. Almost all the giants admit the game is greater than the individual, and that there is always some way they can learn.

This thirst for improvement, though, is not enough in itself. It is simply the fuel for other qualities in the make-up of an outstanding sportsman. These qualities are of equal importance. In Michael Bonallack they are summed up most vividly by an admirer and a friend Charles Lawrie, close observer and supporter of Michael in his successive roles as British captain and chairman of selectors. Charles says, 'Michael is a unique person. He has progressed between Turnberry and Porthcawl because of his sheer determination to do better, backed by tremendous character, tremendous will-power and tremendous will-to-win. His swing is not the most natural the world has ever seen, but nobody has worked harder to improve.'

A further important aspect in the chemistry of this outstanding champion is his reaction to a challenge, be it the broad incentive of a season's golf, with its quota of titles and international appearances, or the more immediate matter of a match or tournament to be won.

The examples come readily. Michael's first national title was the Amateur in 1961. It came in June after the disappointment, a month earlier, of an early exit from the English championship at Wentworth. I recall his wife Angela telling me, 'I have never known him more determined to do well than when he went to Turnberry following his disappointment at Wentworth.'

Michael was then 26. He had been in the top flight four seasons, starting his international appearances in the Walker Cup and England teams of 1957 and reaching the semi-finals of the 1958 Amateur championship, as well as being runner-up for both the English match-play and stroke-play titles in 1959.

After Turnberry Michael felt it his duty to take a major title every season. He began an unbroken series with victory over the tremendously gifted Michael Lunt in the 1962 English championship at Moortown. He kept the title next year at Burnham and Berrow with a demonic short-game display against that classic striker Alan Thirlwell, who looked the champion in every department except in getting the ball in the hole.

Michael was an obvious choice when the British team-builders sharpened their pencils. He followed Minikahda, with Muirfield, Seattle, Turnberry, Baltimore and Royal St. George's in Walker Cup sides. He labelled his clubs for Johannesburg for the 1959 Commonwealth tournament, and played his part in the tie between Britain and Australia in the same event in 1963. He was at Merion when Jack Nicklaus led the United States to victory in the Eisenhower Trophy with the phenonemal 72 holes total of 269. That was in 1960 and two years later came the experience of Kawana in Japan, where good Bonallack scores in the third and fouth rounds helped to keep Britain in their habitual position in the first three. Mexico City, 1966, inevitably followed.

There were battle honours surpassing those of an historic regiment, but Bonallack takes nothing for granted. With the advent of the 1964 season there crop up again the characteristics of built-in modesty and reaction to a challenge. The target for top amateurs was titles, of course ... and Rome, scene of the Eisenhower Trophy world cup in October. Michael came out in May and in his deliberate, devouring stride won the English stroke-play championship for the Brabazon Trophy at Deal. He shattered the opposition with a second round 65, the quality of which no professional in the world could have surpassed. When it was over—and here I come to my point—Michael, the modest, told me, 'I felt I had to do something this season to make sure of getting in the team for Rome.' Such was the challenge and such was his answer.

The situation applies to his greatest season yet, 1965, 'The Year of the Double'. Rome had been something of a disappointment to him. Though Joe Carr led his side to an historic victory, Michael was not satisfied that he had played a full part. Back he went to the drawing board, the test bench and the practice ground. The 'home-work' was well advised.

The 1965 season was a Walker Cup year and, in addition, it was the year of the 'Whizz Kids', Clive Clark, then 19, and Peter Townsend, 18, the teenage terrors who were to prove such a tremendous shot in the arm for golf throughout the land.

Says Michael, 'There was no greater stimulus, no higher incentive, than to keep up with the standard Clive and Peter set in the 1965 season.'

This is what made Mike go. Here was the challenge in the persons of two precocious kids, two talented teenagers who had the effect on amateur golf in the British Isles that Locke and von Nida had on our tournament professionals in the decade after World War II. They were the boys to beat. The teams were harder to make, tournaments harder to win. There was the challenge.

Michael Bonallack's magnificent answer to it was to beat Clive Clark in three epic encounters—in the Amateur and English championships and the no-less-memorable Berkshire Trophy, where Michael shot a fantastic last round of 64 to flatten Clark's challenge as they fought it out head to head.

Clive Clark, perhaps despairing of beating Bonallack, has embraced professionalism! He looks back at his encounters with respect and admiration for Michael. He says, 'What a fine sportsman. What a difficult man to beat. He can still score well if not playing particularly well. His temperament is most impressive. His determination is like iron. Last year I thought he hit the ball better than ever, more solidly. His old fade was gone and he hit it further.

'Michael is just as good in stroke or match play—as his record proves. I'd like to say what an excellent captain he is for the England team. He has the respect of all the team because of his achievements and his example, for his determination and his drive. The spirit in which he plays the game must be an inspiration to everyone around him.'

That is Bonallack the leader. He wins equal acclaim as the member of a team. Joe Carr, the Walker Cup and Eisenhower Trophy captain, says unreservedly, 'Michael as a team man is absolutely marvellous, not simply for his play, but for his effect on the whole team. He usually plays top or near top, but you'll always find him back out with the boys when his match is over, never back in the clubhouse. He's a marvel to have in a team.'

Nobody is closer to Michael than Joe Carr, who has been friend and rival, team-mate and leader, example and companion, over the last decade. Joe says, 'It's his tremendous competitive spirit that makes Michael the man he is.'

Carr agrees that Michael is a better striker now then ever he has been, saying, 'A couple of years ago he had that duck in his swing. He did a tremendous amount of practice to get rid of it. Because of the duck I thought he was not hitting his weight. It is a very important part of the game to be able to hit your weight, because nobody can depend on the short game to pull them through all the time. Michael was getting over this in Rome, now he appears to have got over it completely. He hits the ball with a hook rather than his old slice. I don't think it has made all that difference distance-wise, but it makes a helluva difference psychologically.'

Charles Lawrie, on the evidence of early season obervation of Michael, says, 'I think his technique has improved between Baltimore and now. He hits more behind the ball, more in the back of the ball. But then Michael is improving all the time. He is not content to stand still.

'There is this constant determination to do better. He is the sort of chap who is constantly striving for perfection. He is always trying to add something to his game, and is prepared to work hard to do it. He is not prepared to accept second best.

'As you say, he always rises to a challenge. This again, is character, that tremendous determination and the will to do well. He also has the advantage now of people being frightened of playing him. I don't think there is any doubt about that. They hope they are not in the same quarter... and if they're not in the same half it's better still.'

Michael himself confirms Charles Lawrie's observation on his technique, saying, 'At the Masters I found something I was looking for with regard to hitting behind the ball. Just before I went I had a check-up with John Jacobs and he pointed out I was not hitting behind the ball, but hitting over the top of it. I wasn't aware that when lining up on the target I was aiming a long way right. This let me get my right shoulder very high at the address, with the result that I was not coming into the back of the ball—never really behind it, always over the top of it. Because of aiming too far right, I was bringing my right shoulder over the top of the ball to get the shoulder back on target. My shoulder should have been coming underneath. I could never see the part of the ball I wanted to hit—I could see the top of the ball and not the back.

'It was very noticeable, watching Hogan on the practice field at Augusta—with the first movement of the backswing he turns his head to the right and he is looking at the back of the ball. Jack Nicklaus cocks his chin to the right and has his head a long way behind the ball. He is looking at the back of it. They can get a much bigger shoulder turn, of course, with the chin out of the way.'

Michael's unremitting effort to be a better golfer than he is overlooks no detail. He trains in the winter, watches his weight by dieting, uses his lunch hour to practise at Thorndon Park, close to the family motor-building concern at Basildon in Essex. He does it despite having to admit, 'It becomes harder to find the time. There are added responsibilities at home [he and Angela have three daughters and a son] and in business [he is sales director of an expanding company].'

The matter of equipment receives the same attention. His deadly centre-shaft putter is a faithful friend of many years standing, but he says, 'My drivers are getting progressively lighter—all my clubs are in fact. At one time I had a driver of about 16 oz. In 1961 it was 14 oz. Now I am using one of 13 oz. I think that the important thing is clubhead speed, not weight. The swing weight of my clubs is going down too, as well as the actual weight. It is about D1 or D2.'

In the years between Turnberry, 1961, and Porthcawl, 1965, Michael Bonallack has grown in achievement and in stature but never in the size of his hat. He will remain unaffected by the kind of compliment Charles Lawrie bestows upon him: 'There is something very vital in Michael, something very exciting. He is a great character.'

Joe Carr considers him a better player now than five

years ago... 'Without any shadow of a doubt whatsoever,' says Joe, 'he has improved year by year. Then, I think we mature later over here. We never reach our peak till the age of about 30 or 35. Why, I think I still have a few years' golf left myself [Joe's birth date—February 18th, 1922]. So Michael must have about a century!'

No look into the question of what makes Michael tick would be complete without recording his basic reason for going on and on and up and up in the fiercely competitive sphere he has chosen. 'I enjoy competing,' states Michael baldly.

The golfer who has done everything has one remaining high ambition—to play on a winning British Walker Cup side. It is an ambition every golfer in the British Isles can identify himself with. It befits a splendid champion.

8

Jimmy Hitchcock

IN an Edinburgh hotel room Jimmy Hitchcock sat and looked back on the five years that separated two of his golfing ambitions—his first major tournament win, the Dunlop Masters, in 1960, and his Ryder Cup début at Royal Birkdale.

'Everything seemed to go wrong after I had won the Masters. I had a series of setbacks. I hurt my back twice and had an injury that made my left arm withered and useless. That laid me off tournaments for quite a while.

'This left me feeling like packing it all up at one point. You know how I worked to build my physique after being told as a boy to forget about being a tournament golfer because I was so small and would never hit the ball far enough. When my arm put me out in 1962 I thought, "Oh, no. Have I got to go through all this all over again to get back where I was?" I personally didn't want to do it. I was ready to go to South Africa and get a job in business.

'But my wife Nancy made me change my mind. She said, "I think it is worth it. Try it again. Give it another go."'

Jimmy's wife got her way. And took such a share in the uphill struggles that realised Hitchcock's boyhood dream of playing for Britain against America that he says, 'Without Nancy's help I would never have done it.'

Nancy Hitchcock, of course, is Jimmy's partner in

every sense of the word. They met on his first tour of South Africa in 1961. She was Nancy Rohm, star of women's golf in her own country. She came to England and married Jimmy in 1963. Then she turned professional and became her husband's assistant at Ashford Manor, Middlesex, gaining admittance to the Professional Golfers' Association. Her deep knowledge of the golf swing and knack of fault-spotting and gift for instruction combine to make Nancy a huge success as a teacher.

Life as a tournament golfer has always been tough for Jimmy Hitchcock. He had to battle with a highly-strung, nervous temperament, as well as an hereditary lack of inches and muscle. It looked as though he had broken both barriers when that Masters victory came in 1960. But he had to wait another five years before making his first Ryder Cup appearance at 35—an age at which his contemporaries Peter Alliss and Bernard Hunt were veterans of six appearances. Jim had to wait almost as long for his second tournament success in Britain, the 1965 Agfa-Geveart at Stoke Poges.

The stony path to renewed success has been one of tortuous training of body and of mind. Jimmy gives his wife first credit for anything he has achieved. Then he thanks a correspondence course which has trained his mind and equipped him mentally for the pressures of life and tournament golf. Thirdly he intensified his pre-season physical training to a degree that would do credit to an Olympics athlete.

Jimmy remains a modest, humble person, giving generous thanks to people and things that have helped him on his way. But in the final count it was he himself who punished his body, disciplined his mind and hit the golf shots. His story is a triumph of perseverance and character. Jimmy begins it with the case history of the greatest setback in the course of the five-year pause in his career, the arm injury which was not even yet mended, with consequent affect on his hitting power.

'After the Masters 1961 was not too bad really. I had some thirds, seconds, fifths in tournaments—things like that. I won a tournament in South Africa on my second tour there. Then in April 1962 came the injury to my arm. I did it in the pro-am. preceding the Cox Moore tournament. I hit a tree-root in playing a shot. Continued playing and thought no more of it. But next morning I woke up and could not move my arm. It was useless. I literally could not move it at all. It was paralysed. I had to pick up my left arm with my right to put it in a shirt or coat. When I got out of bed this arm just fell limp. I saw a doctor and a physiotherapist at once. But nothing could be done.

'I went home and saw more doctors, manipulators and people like that. Eventually I had to go and see a friend called Mr. Ward, a surgeon who is a member at Wentworth. An X-ray revealed I had pinched the skin on a nerve. Golf was out for three months. It was 10 weeks before I could get any sort of power back at all. I tried to play in the Yorkshire Evening News tournament. I found myself hitting a driver as far as a three-iron; at the 18th, only a drive and five-iron to a moderate hitter, I was still short after two full woods. It was ridiculous. I went home thinking, "I'll have to try more practice and exercises." But I was told exercise would not help. Rest was the only thing. Chick Dixon, the Dunlop representative, had something similar through a shrapnel wound and he said it would take two or three years to get right again. Well, over three years have gone and I'm not right now really. My left arm is much smaller in the bicep and the forearm than my right. It used to be bigger than the right.

'The next two seasons were still not good. So at the end of 1964 I thought the next thing to do was to buy some equipment and really get down to hard training right through the winter. The only thing you have to be careful of if you train hard is not to get musclebound. So I bought myself a vibrator, a big thing that you stand in. It cost £70. Its purpose was to keep me supple. I did not get heavy weights, only these two 10 lb. hand weights which I carry with me all the time. At home I have a static bicycle, a great thing for strengthening the legs, and a stomach board. I spent well over a £100 altogether. I have not become very muscular; all I've done is get wiry and strong. Not so strong as I used to be. My hands are strong but the left arm is the weakness. Towards the end of a tournament the left wrist begins to give a bit and the club turns over instead of going through the ball. I am working on the left arm all the time.

'The hardest time was when I started to play again after stopping for 10 weeks. I ached everywhere. All my golf muscles had lost their tone. I was stiff in every muscle. I used to walk miles every day when my arm was bad, and do leg and trunk exercises. But it was no good if you had nothing to hit with, nothing to control the club. I began again with ladies' clubs, my wife's. Then light men's clubs. Special light woods. That was when I could hardly face it, building up all over again.'

Jimmy was stiffened in his resolve to continue his body-building and be patient about his wasted arm by the course in applied psychology he took through the post. This began early in 1964. He was thumbing through a *Reader's Digest* and came upon a pamphlet advertising the course. He had in the past tried hypnosis and thought transference to discipline nerves that reached screaming point in the course of tournament play. He read the pamphlet to Nancy. She urged him to try it.

'That course has helped me so much. It has taught me to have faith and given me the belief that I was getting stronger. Some of the teachings are so applicable to golf. I carry bits and pieces round with me to read if things are not going too well on the course.' Here Jimmy pulled out from his hip pocket a score-card covered with notes. 'Listen to this,' he continued, '"I am strong, dominant, bound to succeed, born for victory, nothing can deter me from my purpose." ... Now this is a thing I think is good for all sportsman. Here are some more ... "Obstacles but fire my will to win ... Discouragements prod me on ... All men are my friends whether friend or foe; my friends encourage me, my foes stimulate me."'

Jimmy broke off to talk about a famous player, of whom he said, 'He was the one man I hated, and I know he feels the same about me. But after reading this stuff you feel different. For one thing, hate is no good. It only comes back at you. But this fellow, now I think he's just the same as I am—he's only trying to do to me what I'm trying to do to him on the golf course. I know he doesn't like me and that makes me want to do well. My foes stimulate me, you see.'

Then a return to the texts of Positive Thinking... '"My superiors must respect my sincerity, integrity and ability... I believe in myself and my task, hence I bow to no man... My motto—"I can, I will ... walk with success, I will succeed. Success is certain. I am success." If things are going wrong I turn to my card and read them.'

He showed me one of the textbooks, *Life Triumphant*, by Henry Knight Miller. The chapter headings included: Auto-suggestion, Fear and Worry Vanquished. He continued in his frank, expressive way: 'When I first started reading, I didn't understand this stuff. But by the time you have read halfway through a volume you start acting these things. You know, like Eric Brown, the way he used to walk around—swaggering, arrogant, head in the air. The way Dai Rees always walks. Always the perky little

Cock Robin. I think that's why he's been as good as he is all these years.'

Thumbing through his manual of success, Jimmy continued, at machine-gun pace: 'Now here's a thing that struck me so much I made it into a sign 18 in. high and 9 in. wide and stuck it on my bedroom wall:

A QUITTER NEVER WINS, A WINNER NEVER QUITS

'It's amazing, you know, I can wake up feeling, "Oh, I don't want to exercise today." Then my eyes catch those words facing me across the room, and you cannot but get out of bed. It's a challenge. Before you know what you've done, you've hopped straight out and you're at it.

'Of all the things I've tried—hypnotism, relaxation, and thought transference—this is the most effective, the course I'm doing now.

'I have changed my whole way of life through it. I am a better person to live with. I have learned how to think correctly. To cut out hate. It has the most effect on me because I actively work on it myself. I read it, I absorb it.

'When I first started the course I thought, "This is ridiculous, I am going to cut out everything" ... Then I found it tells you the way to do it. Make up rhymes, slogans and sayings. To think that everything that happens is for the best. I used to sit around brooding over things, thinking "Gee, I haven't qualified. My world has fallen in." Now I feel this is something to urge me on, to make me go.

'I had to wait four hours at Little Aston wondering whether I had qualified for the Martini—just after I'd won at Stoke Poges—but it wasn't the agony it used to be. I had these things to think about, the bright side, that there must be some good in it. I used to stay awake nights thinking things like, "I'm playing with so-and-so tomorrow and he hits the ball miles past me." Now if anything comes into my head like that I've got something to counteract it—some thought or saying which does not permit fear, depression or worry.

'I'll give you an example. The day before the little Ryder Cup match in the Senior Service some of the boys were saying in the locker room what it's like to play in your first Ryder Cup. You can't tee the ball on the peg for nerves, and all that sort of thing. Well, I said to myself, if I'm going to feel like that I'd rather not play. So I made the small Ryder Cup game a test. I told myself it was going to be something terrifically thrilling, something marvellous, people there to watch. Not something terrible, an ordeal. It worked. I really enjoyed it. It was thrilling.

'If only I could describe what it was like when I first used to play in tournaments. Gee, it used to kill me. I'd get out there and feel "I'll never hit this ball." I was so wound up. We had old Hugh Docherty in those days as starter. He used to help quite a lot. He knew how I felt and would relax me with remarks about the weather, and how bad some well-known player had hit his first shot.'

Was Jimmy still in this state when he gained that first big success in the Masters? 'I think I was. I'll tell you what happened then. Shortly before the Masters in 1960 I played with Henry Longhurst—he had been invited by my club captain—and he told me at the time, "You strike the ball better than anyone since Henry Cotton." Then he mentioned it in an article, and just before the start of the Masters took the trouble to come to me and say, "This is your tournament. Nobody here is good enough to beat you." It was a piece of psychology, I suppose. It made me feel, "If a great authority like that can say this, then I am not thinking enough of myself." Dick Burton used to tell me the same... "The trouble with you is you don't know how good you are. You don't believe in yourself."

'How do you learn to believe in yourself? Positive thought is the answer. Take giving a lesson. Most people tell you what you are doing wrong. My belief in giving a lesson is to tell a fellow what he should do right, not what he's doing wrong.

'Another thing is the Ryder Cup in 1959. I was eighth in the averages and I'd have earned my place really if it had been the present system. But I didn't get in. Of course, if ever I hated anybody it was then. I hated the world. I thought everybody was against me. I had a chip on my shoulder and hated everything and everybody that walked.

'What this all did, now I realise, was to make me go. That winter I went to South Africa and met my wife. The best thing that's happened to me. Next year I won the Masters and another tournament the following winter in South Africa.

'The part Nancy has played has been terrific. She has watched me hit golf balls now for years and years and years. She knows my weaknesses. If it was possible for her to carry the bag for me I don't think I would have hit many bad shots. She is always ready with a little word, particularly about my habit of having a little look before the ball is off the ground. I get away from it very quickly. "Stay with the ball," she is always drumming into me.

'Putting we've worked on for hours together, I bought a special carpet, grass green, very good quality, laid in the bedroom. We have worked for hours together putting on that. We still do. I putt on the carpet every night.

'A thing you have to consider when you are doing a course like I am is what a help it is to have someone doing it with you. It wouldn't be half as good trying to do this on your own. You really want some help, and Nancy did it all. She has spent hours working with me, she stood over me, she trained me. When I got the books Nancy said, "Right, we'll read them out loud. They tell you to do this, so that you get it into your head." I used to read most of it to her.'

Jimmy has armed himself with the teachings of his course to give himself a better temperament for life and for golf. His moods and depressions are banished. His tension and vulnerable feelings are no longer part of him. Jingles and rhymes guide him to cheerfulness and confidence. When his arm was mending slowly he would repeat, 'Day by day in every way my arm is getting stronger and stronger. Day by day in every way' . . . and so on *ad infinitum.*

'The value of repeating these things over and over is that while you are doing so it is difficult to think of anything else. The mind can only take one thing at a time.' says Jimmy. 'I use it between golf shots. If I go in the rough I make up a saying that tells me it won't be lieing badly. With those putts I line them up and repeat, "Second by second, I am holing these putts better and better." *It fills your mind with positive thought.*

'I was under great pressure in the Esso tournament which settled the Ryder Cup places. But with my new attitude I started off like a bomb. Then I went to sleep in the locker room for two hours between matches and took 41 to the turn after I had done 67, 67, 67. That was something I learned. Another thing I did wrong was to think about the points instead of about playing the course. And I should never have driven from home across London every day. I should have stayed at a hotel and cut out that 20 hours' driving. You have to concentrate so when you're driving.

'Getting in the Ryder Cup team has done me the world

of good, I feel a different person now that I am in. I feel a terrific weight has been lifted off my shoulders.

'Now that I realise how hard it is to get in the side, really and truly I know I was not ready in 1959. It would only have needed one of the boys to start saying what was ahead of us out there, and I would have been like a jelly. I am nervous still. But I can control my nerves now. I feel if I do happen to hit a shot into a bush, then it was meant to be, it was fate. I would not carry on expecting it at every hole, as I used to do.

'I enjoy my golf now. I used to hate it. Gee I used to hate playing tournaments... Till I knew about the sort of thing I study now. Now the game is a test, a challenge. In the old days I'd moan over a bad lie; now I look at it as a test of skill.'

You must take off your hat to Jimmy Hitchcock. They don't come franker or more honest. As for work, he's in the Ben Hogan-Gary Player class.

9
Harold Henning

MUCH travelled Harold Henning is one of the British golf scene's most faithful summer migrants. Just how familiar a figure is the lanky South African a story from the 1966 Open at Muirfield shows. Harold played the final round with Dave Thomas. His gallery included his charming English wife Pat and a couple of friends. At one stage of the round this small group stood behind a keen little band of Scottish matrons. One of the ladies knowledgeably passed the information to her friends: 'You know, this Harold Henning has been coming here for years. He has even got two young sons on the circuit, Alan and Graham.'

Harold collapsed into peals of laughter as he recounted this priceless story against himself. He has indeed been a long-term visitor to British shores, making an exploratory trip in 1955, and never missing a season since he brought with him the South African Open and six provincial titles in his golden year of 1957. But Harold's career started so early—at 18 he had won his first big tournament—that even now (1967) he is only 32. His only son Hanley is in fact five and a half years old! Brothers Graham, the fair one, is 25 and Alan, who wears spectacles, 23. There is, incidentally, another golf pro brother, Brian, 29, who has a club job and has not yet been to Britain.

Harold Henning, the epitome of the jet-age, globe-trotting tournament professional, has never been a controversial figure. But he has always made news. He is the kind of fellow who prefers to let his golf clubs do the talking. And they have—with seven wins in eight South African tournaments in 1957 which prefaced his first serious season in the United Kingdom. With a string of successes in Britain in 1958; third place in the Centenary Open. And most sensational of all, the £10,000 hole-in-one in the 1963 Esso Golden tournament.

It was strange, therefore, to find Harold the centre of a situation in which he was virtually driven back to the European circuit following his most successful attack ever on the American circuit.

At San Antonio in May 1966 he won the Texas Open, his first win in America, one which made him a member of the very small band of overseas players to break into the travelling Fort Knox which is the U.S. tour. Harold harvested some $30,000 (over £10,000) in two months in the States. Then the U.S. Professional Golfers' Association told him the welcome had run out. Abruptly the door was slammed. He was told the only way he could play in America again was to attend the newly inaugurated annual school for tournament players and through it qualify for an Approved Tournament Players' card.

But for this the British and European tournaments would not have seen much of Harold in 1966. So, after playing in the rich Carling world championship when it came to Royal Birkdale, Harold rested for a month at home and ended his year playing it according to the P.G.A. of America rule book—by going back to school! He sat through classes which spelled out the facts of tournament life by the side of the 'rookies' for whom the project was designed. Then the P.G.A. chiefs showed excellent grace by excusing him the examination of playing the 144-hole tournament, the test to which his brother Alan and all the other students were subjected.

Harold's presence in the Florida class was richly ironic, for he is a hardened circuit performer who has played and won tournaments in a score of different countries, has shared Canada Cup victory with Gary Player (1965) finishing second, and three times third in the event besides, and in a brief sojourn leapt to the top bracket of dollar earners in U.S.A.

After a dozen years on the world's fairways, which have always yielded him a fair living, Harold Henning has now reached his peak. When we talked during a pause in the tournament rounds of summertime Harold was able to say without any bombast and with customary matter-of-fact tones: 'In the past 12 months I have won 10 tournaments. In 1966 up to now I have played in 22 and won five, finished second three or four times, and been third in three or four others.'

Against this background of current happenings Harold talked frankly about himself. About the downs as well as the present upswing in his affairs, for there was a spell not so long ago when things were not going at all right for him. We met at tournament player Bill Large's flat at Radlett, near St. Albans, in itself evidence of the camaraderie which exists among the globe-trotting golfers. Bill was doing the Continental tour, Harold was staying behind for the Esso tournament. What more natural than the Henning family to keep the Large home occupied?

The most significant thing Harold said was to underline his decision to make the American circuit the centre of his activities. When I brought up his future plans he said: 'I shall play most of my golf in America in future, I shan't play too much in Britain, much as I like playing here. It is simply that the rewards here are not big enough for me. At my stage I have got to start thinking where I can make the most money. Having found I can make far more money in the States, it would be pointless not to try for more now my golf is good enough.

'I did say at one time British conditions suited my game better than American. But that was some years ago. Britain suited my game in the respect that I could make a living here. I am playing well enough now to know that I can do well in America, so I must go over there.

'I know that in a good year in the States I can make more than I can in five years in Britain. The tax situation is more favourable there too; comparatively light, because they allow you far more expenses than they do in Britain. In a full year I would probably make $50,000 or $60,000 in prize money playing like I am this year. But over and above that you are going to make a lot more on the side, in endorsements and things like that. So your $50,000 or $60,000 would become $100,000 [£35,000].

'No, you don't have to win the Masters or the Open to make this kind of money. You only have to win one tournament to really set yourself up. Finishing in the top 50 money winners counts for everything, it's the big thing. Do that and you're IN. You can't help but make money. There are so many bits and pieces.'

Harold's victory in the Texas Open, second place at Dallas, and sackful of dollars puts him in the class of other invaders to have made their mark in the States—Bruce Crampton, Bruce Devlin and Kel Nagle of Australia, New Zealand's Bob Charles, and, of course, Gary Player. He sees his future mapped as some 20 tournaments a year in U.S., spread over a six months' stay, four months at home in South Africa, and short excursions elsewhere, including Britain. 'I shall continue to play in the British Open, although it is not a tournament I play in thinking I can win it. I don't have a tremendous record on seaside courses, despite my win in the Pringle tournament at Carnoustie [1964]. Being tall and skinny I have never stood up to strong winds. But as you say there might be another year like Bob Charles's at Lytham in 1963. He is like me, slim, not built for a wind.'

Earlier, Harold had talked about the lean years, the spell between winning the Sprite tournament at Selsdon Park in 1960 and going without another success in Britain until the 1964 Pringle. 'In those three years I think I won only two tournaments—from 1961 to 1963. Even in South Africa I didn't do any good. I was driving badly and my putting, which was the strong point of my game, came back to very ordinary. Before that I could get away with playing badly. My putting covered a multitude of sins. When my putting left me I was really very ordinary. When I did start to play better, driving better and hitting better shots all round, then my putting came back as well. I suppose it went because of all the pressure I was placing on it.'

Harold had the break of a lifetime at Moor Park in July 1963—what he freely admitted was a 'fluke' golf shot which netted him the £10,000 hole-in-one prize in the Esso tournament. This fortune was split three ways, by prior agreement, with Denis Hutchinson and Brian Lundie, fellow South African players. 'Hutch' was playing in the tournament; Brian was acting as Harold's caddie, 'for the experience'.

Harold admits that this giant slice of luck had a profound effect on his golf. 'It gave me a much better frame of mind, knowing I did not have to go out there and play for the next meal.' The revival in his form began almost at once. He went to the Continent and finished up tieing for the Swiss Open. He lost the play-off to Dai Rees, but it was the best performance since an isolated success in the 1962 South Africa Open.

The year 1964 was the first of three which have got progressively better. 'I was playing good golf before I won the Pringle tournament at Carnoustie,' Harold points out. 'I won the Danish Open, only a small tournament, but from a very good field, and I won by 10 or 11 shots.' In the same year Harold won the Swiss Open for the second time. He thinks 1965 was an even better year.... 'Particularly towards the end. I started playing well after the British Open, which I had to miss because of the death of my mother. I came back to Europe and won the German and Swiss, and the Canada Cup for South Africa, with Gary Player in Madrid.'

About this time, too, came the small but significant success in America which sparked off Harold's 1966 pillage of the U.S. tour. Harold said: 'In 1965 I didn't make the cut in the Masters, but in the Carling I made $2,000 [£714] in one week. This made me realise that you can make money in the States on courses other than Augusta, which is a course that requires special skill and preparation.'

It was this useful pick-up which gave Harold the encouragement to go back to America. Harold explained: 'People have said in the past why don't I go to the States. I have been reluctant because I didn't think I could make a living there. I thought the standard was too high and I was content to play where I knew I could make a living. The expense there is pretty terrific, and I didn't think I could play that well. So when I did win in Texas it was very self-satisfying.'

Harold made his first excursion to U.S. in 1956, when only 21, and finished third at Fort Wayne. He went to the States most years from 1959 on, and has played in the Masters at Augusta most years since. As British players have found, the Masters is not a tournament at which you can drop in for the week.

'On the few occasions I acquitted myself reasonably well I was over there a month beforehand,' Harold said. 'In other words, I went soon enough to give myself a chance. The difference between a good shot and a bad shot at Augusta National is a couple of feet. That's all it takes to turn a shot from a birdie to a bogey. In 1966, for example, I got there from the Far East at the top of my form, but I arrived only the same week, so I didn't go any good. The next week I played and did reasonably well, the third week I was second at Dallas, and the fourth I won in Texas. So it takes you a month to adjust and acclimatise and get into your real form in America.'

Harold went on to put forward the reasons his game, which he once thought not good enough for America, had raised itself to the standard of a tournament winner in the States. 'The sort of game I've got at the moment will suit any sort of conditions,' he said. 'My game is better all round than it was five years ago. My driving is better, so are my iron shots. I concentrate a bit better. I was way out mentally five years ago. I did not know what I was trying to do.

'Maybe it's because I'm a bit older, more mature, more experienced. I don't make the rash mistakes I did in the past, or hit the loose shots. Slash a drive 30 yards off line, or go into the bushes and run up a seven or a nine. I could never complete four rounds without having one mediocre or really bad round in it. Sometimes, I'd be playing well enough to get away with this and still win tournaments. But nowadays you can't do that.

'Now I seem capable of stringing four rounds together more consistently. I do it by not getting flustered, or worried into making stupid mistakes. It is very easy to make foolish mistakes and run up a bad score, but that doesn't happen too often any more. I think better. It comes with experience, I suppose. I know how to hold my game together much better than I did.'

What about your game, has that changed? I asked Harold. 'My driving is better, more consistent, but my swing has not changed enough for anyone to notice it. But I have lived with it so long that I know what to do so that there is a 90 per cent chance of making a good hit at the ball. I used to sort of hit and hope. I was never quite sure whether I was in the correct position or not. I have learned through trial and error, through playing every week. Advice from others is all very well, but playing your own game week after week is the best answer to your own problems.'

Is it still harder to win in the States than anywhere else? 'Now that I have won there I feel that I could win again. The week before I won in San Antonio, I should have won the tournament at Dallas. I didn't because I still had a bit of stage fright there. I just could not believe I was in this position . . . leading by two shots with the last round to come. I said to myself, "Hell, it looks as though you're going to win a tournament here." These thoughts put me off a bit. I made a few silly mistakes in the last round which I would never have made if the tournament had been anywhere else but in America.

'The following week when I was in the same position, I knew by then that this wasn't an accident. So I just went on and won.'

Harold has won tournaments in a dozen or more countries. During 1966 he won on three continents. How do you adjust to what must be utterly different conditions? 'To me now there are no conditions that are utterly different or strange. I can go and play in the street, as it were. It is just that I have played all over the world for so many years. A month before I won in Texas I won in the Far East, and

I had never played the circuit there, except for the 1957 Canada Cup in Tokyo.

'Playing the Far East is really an experience. There is tremendous heat; the courses are different, and far from good; the food is strange and not at all to my taste. It is a terrific adjustment to make. Unless you are accustomed to travelling and living in different countries you just can't play there. I know from the experience of the Canada Cup that the fellows who come from different countries and are not usually travellers, they just can't adjust to the food, the climate, the time, and different things like that. I don't have any trouble like that. I played well in the Far East. I won one, came second in one, and third in another. It does not take a great deal for me to adjust, having had all this experience.

'This is a thing that strikes me about British players. The only way they can expect to compete at world-wide level is to go out and get the experience. I am surprised that more do not play in the Continental tournaments. That is a very good starting point for travelling and getting the essential experience.

'I don't think that the standard of the top British players has improved as it should have done in the past few years. There is nobody outstanding, and the same applies to the young players. There is no youngster who really impresses me.

'In the States there are any amount of good players. They are coming up all the time. The "Big Three" *don't* have it their own way. We are misled by the Masters, which Nicklaus, Palmer and Player have been winning so often. Nicklaus should win it every year, because the course is built entirely to suit his game.

'I am a great believer in horses for courses. Over in the States, and even in Britain, a lot of players don't go to some of the tournaments because the courses don't suit them. The tournaments are played on almost the same courses every year and the players know which they can play well. Some are good driving courses, a bit narrow. Others are wide open. So the players pick their weeks according to their game. They take time off if it is not their kind of course. Not everybody plays the full circuit, they pick and choose their tournaments. It's the accepted thing. Neither the "Big Three" nor anybody else is going to monopolise the tour any more, there are too many good players.'

So 'Harold the Horse'—as Henning is affectionately known on the circuit—has picked as his courses the tough but rewarding American tour. He feels he is now ready to tackle the New World of golf and share its overflowing coffers.

There are a score of morals in this long look at Harold Henning, one of the most complete professionals tournament golf in my time has known. Not least is that it takes time; a long, long time to find completeness as a tournament golfer. The genius that brings early success to the like of Jack Nicklaus or Gary Player is rare. The long slog, the peaks and valleys, the rough road—these are the everyman's way to the top. Travel, travel, travel. Play, play, play. In time Britain may produce a winner on the American circuit. But it will be done only by doing it the Harold Henning way.

The administrators of the British circuit, as well as the players, should ponder on Henning's departure. Over here we can ill afford the 'star drain'. There is much rationalisation to be done if the British circuit is to maintain its place as the second most important in the world.

The locker rooms will not be quite the same without the throaty chuckle of Harold Henning, downing a lager and dragging at yet another cigarette. Coombe Hill member Wally Dubabney, close friend and great fan of the lanky

Springbok, said to me: 'If you are writing about Harold you should entitle the story "The Nice Guy who Doesn't Come Last".'

It is hard to improve on that—and I find this very tough, taking ideas from an 'amateur'!

10
Bernard Hunt

THERE may be other great seasons for him, but 1963 will always be known as 'The Year of Bernard Hunt'.

Peter Alliss started this. In his perceptive way Peter said: 'Bernard hasn't been given half the credit he deserves for what he has done this season.' It was at one of the less frenzied moments of the tournament trail. The golf talk flowed gently with the after-lunch coffee in that stately home of golf, the mansion clubhouse of Moor Park, on the eve of the Esso Round Robin tournament.

Inevitably the cash-collecting deeds of Bernard Hunt cropped up. Woodbrook, 1963, had marked Ben's fourth four-figure victory of the year, something that had never been done before in a single season. His winnings had passed Peter Thomson's 1962 record of £5,764. Before the week was out he was once more to be involved in a big-money finish, sharing second place to Kel Nagle with Peter Thomson and Harry Weetman. His take for the season was to reach £7,209, then a record for the British circuit.

Bernard had won the Swallow-Penfold, Gevacolor, Dunlop Masters and Sweet Afton events—with aggregates of 272, 273, 282 and 270. Simple arithmetic puts this at 55 under fours, and a further calculation makes it 39 under par. In addition there were facile first places in two smaller tournaments, and joint fourths in the Schweppes P.G.A. and Martini events. And when we come to the much lamented showing of home players in the 1963 Open championship, Bernard's 11th-place tie did make him the first *Englishman*, with Christy O'Connor the only Ryder Cup team-mate to head him.

For my part, Peter Alliss's point was well taken. Had any overseas player plundered the British circuit in the manner of Hunt he would have been hailed as a destroyer, wrecker, genius or what have you. It has happened in not-so-distant years. The villains of the piece, from the home viewpoint, have successively been Bobby Locke, Norman von Nida, and Peter Thomson. Rarely has a native golfer dominated the professional circuit in the manner of 'Big Ben'. Fred Daly in 1947-8, and maybe Charles Ward in 1948-9, Dai Rees in the early 50s or Christy O'Connor in 1959 to 1962 have stood out from their fellows as prolific money winners. But not in the golden vein of Bernard John Hunt in 1963.

The rewards today are, of course, much greater. But then so is the competition. If America's circuit is the world's toughest, then Britain's, however far behind, must take second place. After all, it can boast Gary Player and Bob Charles as its star graduates. So there is no denying that the king of this circuit, the Master, in fact, merits all the bouquets to come his way.

It is next door to a golfing cliché to look for the 'secret' behind every success story. But if you expect to find this nonsense with blunt Ben Hunt then you will probe in vain. Nothing changes about Bernard. He is still the most modest and reticent of fellows, still the master of understatement. Just as careful and saving with his words as with his golf shots.

In all the years I have known him his most overworked phrase has been, 'I was very steady'. It covered anything from a 70 in a high gale to a record 63 at Wentworth's East Course. Now that he is winning so often there has to be a slight modification, 'A few putts went in.' The tone is the same, and the expression of seriousness. Certainly there is the same avoidance of fuss. Bernard always underplays his hand. Bernard's colleagues of the circuit admire and envy his success—though not one begrudges it—they are almost as brief as Bernard in their attempts to explain his boom season. Peter Alliss says, 'His game looks exactly the same. I play with him in exhibitions almost every week-end, have done for several seasons. Nothing is different this year.'

I turned, therefore, to those closest to Ben in an attempt to fathom his mood, method, approach or whatever it was that grooved the winning ways of 1963. The firm of John Hunt and Sons (Golfers) Ltd. has always been a close-knit outfit ever since the principals of it came out of the little nine-hole course at Atherstone in the heart of England to take the first steps to fame around 1953. It is a family firm in the full sense of the word. Ben and his brother Geoff rode the circuit together. Bernard's wife Margaret follows him whenever the duties of raising a young family of three permit, and she has been to South Africa and the West Indies doing it. His parents, John and Lilian Hunt, use their days off from the shop at Hartsbourne Country Club to watch Bernard and Geoff whenever there is a big tournament close to London. They know Ben if anyone does. Their views are interesting—and varied.

Margaret Hunt in the course of an afternoon off at Moor Park said: 'I think Bernard is only now getting his due reward for all the hard work he has put into his game. For several seasons he has been near the top without winning as often as he looked like doing. He became a bit of a "champion runner-up". He would come home after being in the lead and not staying there, very despondent about his luck. Perhaps it was bad luck, perhaps not. This year everything has gone well. One win can give you enormous confidence. I believe that has happened to Bernard. I don't know any single fact that would really explain it. The closest I can get to it is that all things are coming off at once when Bernard plays.'

Bernard's mother, Mrs. Lilian Hunt, was in charge of the shop at Hartsbourne while her husband and Geoff were on the course when I spoke to her. Mrs. Hunt's life has been golf. One of her brothers is Bill Firkins, the Stourbridge pro. Her home for many years was on the Atherstone course. She recalled those days when she said: 'I remember when Bernard was 12 years old he was reading a golf book by Henry Cotton and he said, "This is how I'm going to earn my living, Mum." I didn't dream he'd make the words come true the way he has. But he has always been very serious and hardworking about his golf. You know that terrible winter we had? Well, it did not stop Bernard and Geoff from practising. As soon as there was a clear patch of fairway they went out and hit balls to each other. Bernard seemed very determined about doing well this year.'

John Hunt returned from a teaching stint to tell me first: 'Bernard is concentrating better. He is getting more "with it" about his own game and forgetting what the others are doing. Look at Ben Hogan, that was his way. He would play the course and ignore the opposition. The example is there for everyone, but it is easier to see the right thing than to do it. But if you are trying along the right lines then suddenly it can register. You can't account for it. How, why or when. It is just one of those things.'

John went on to confirm that Bernard is reaping the long-term benefits of his great industry. 'Another thing may be that all the hours of practice are paying off. No one practises harder than Bernard. I have known him arrive at the course at 10, bash away all the morning, come back again in the afternoon, and again in the evening.'

Finally, John Hunt, a great student of the golf swing, said of Bernard's game: 'He has developed a method of his own and stuck to it. We are so gullible in this game, aren't we? Ready to try anything. Bernard has been told time and time again how much better he would be if swung more upright. He has steadfastly stuck to his own method. As I see his swing, he keeps the wrists straight on the backswing. The wrist cock comes as he starts the downswing. You don't see the shaft go over at the top of the backswing. He cocks the wrists at the start of the pull down. It puts him in the same position as anyone else at the start of the impact area, and, of course, ensures a late hit. That is what makes him such a good iron player.'

Geoff Hunt, six years the junior of Bernard (born February 2nd, 1930), brought the outlook of the tournament player to the question. Geoff, national assistants' champion at 18, had his career halted by a long illness, but reached Ryder Cup rank in 1963. Geoff's theory is: 'I think Ben's good season is because he had much more rest last winter. No tour to America or Jamaica. He was forced to relax in the winter and that built up a will to win and the reserves of nervous energy winning requires. The Open championship was a disappointment because he overplayed himself beforehand. He had no choice because tournaments follow one another so quickly at that time. But after winning the Masters he had to go back to the Bowmaker and then travel up to St. Annes. If there had been time to go and relax in between he would have done better. In the early practice rounds Ben played just as he had been all the season. Then when it counted I thought he showed a bit of mental tiredness. . . .'

Geoff went on to detail the one slight change in Bernard's game his close observations had detected. 'Ben went through a period when he faded the ball. He stood very open, as though he was aiming to the left. In the last two years he has squared up his stance and the ball flies straighter.'

I put it to Geoff: 'The essential difference in Ben is not so much in his game as his mental outlook. In the last three or four seasons he has been in a position to win tournaments more times than any other single British player. He would play the first two rounds brilliantly, or even the first three. Then he would drop back on the third or fourth round.' Geoff agreed and said: 'Threatening to win and winning is a phase you have got to go through. Your thinking does not alter overnight. You just go on trying and eventually break through whatever the mental block is that makes you a near-winner instead of a winner.'

Dave Thomas, close colleague of Bernard's and one of the weekly England-Wales exhibition foursome, confirms most of what has been said. Dave puts it this way: 'I have always thought Ben was good. Now everything is going right for him together. He is playing four good rounds a tournament instead of three. He hits his irons as well as anyone in the game and nobody has putted well more consistently. For a long time he has had the attitude of thinking "I'm satisfied to finish in the first three". But once he won he seemed to get the flavour for it. Technically there is no change in his game.'

This view ties up exactly with that of Henry Cotton, who says: 'Obviously Bernard has made a breakthrough in temperament. He has got used to winning. His method is something I have dreamed of and written about for years—swing waist-high and still hit the ball 300 yards. Cuts down the margin of error. But strong hands are vital.'

Neil Coles partnered his new Canada Cup team-mate in his first big win of the season at Ayr. Neil says: 'I have not played with Bernard a lot but I was impressed with his composure on the course. He appears very calm. He does not get flustered easily.' Yes, there is a touch of the Sphinx-like attitude of Locke and Charles about Hunt.

Harold Henning, the man who passed Hunt's winnings for the season in a single stroke which won Esso's Golden £10,000 jackpot for an ace, has also brought in Bernard as a winner. Harold observes: 'Bernard is having a spell with his putter, but that is not all. You have got to hit the ball into putting range and that is where he scores. His wedge play is so good. He rarely misses a putt from 10 feet in. This makes him ruthless on short courses. He gives himself so many opportunities. His long game has not changed at all. He is no longer frightened of winning. When a man gets into that frame of mind he just keeps on. How to get there? I don't suppose he could tell you himself.'

And he couldn't. Harold Henning was right about that. 'There's no answer. It is just the way these things go,' said Bernard when taxed about the recipe for the season's success. 'I haven't played any better than in other years. The difference between winning and losing is nothing. You can't put your finger on it. It might be just a matter of holing the odd putt at the right time. That can get you going. I have not found any secret, I can assure you. Nothing new, nothing at all.'

Watching Bernard win has, however, revealed new aspects of the man. Take that crushing final round of 65 at Ayr. It was ruthless. Hunt appeared to take the course by the scruff of the neck and wring a good score out of it. He subdued Belleisle. He went out in 31. His 65 was the best of the day by three strokes. He won by nine shots.

At Stoke Poges I detected another new quality—the resilience so characteristic of Peter Thomson at his peak, the ability to hit back immediately after a reverse instead of folding and losing. Ben had a six early in that final round. It was followed at the next hole by a two. When he three-putted the 10th, he at once holed from six yards for a two at 11. In the Masters play-off he lost the first hole to Ralph Moffitt's birdie. But the next three birdies of the play-off all belonged to the ruthless Hunt. He smashed into the lead at Woodbrook with a third-round 64 which caused Harry Weetman to say: 'It made my 68 look pretty sick.' Hunt lashed himself for bad golf and missed chances at Lytham. A week later he had turned that anger into the golden shots of Woodbrook.

Straighter driving. Masterly irons. A putting streak. A breakthrough in temperament. Reward for hard work. Unflappability. Perfection of a method. Experience. The taste for winning . . . all these parts obviously fit into the whole which made Bernard John Hunt Britain's master golfer and master money-making golfer of 1963. Above all towers the character of the man—unchanging, apparently unchangeable. Bernard is still the industrious, sincere and humble golfer one has always known him to be. These are the qualities, admirable and essential, for the man who wants success from the most elusive, most tantalising and most humbling of all games.

There are no last words on the subject more revealing than ever-modest Bernard's own . . . 'The courses have suited me.'

Typical.

11

Cobie Legrange

COBIE LEGRANGE shook success firmly by the hand one recent English summer. The frank-eyed and patently sincere young man from South Africa talked about his triumphant invasion of Britain and the Continent before he left to continue his globe-trotting in Australia and New Zealand to round out his golfing year. His peak, of course, was winning the Dunlop Masters on the classic Royal Birkdale links in a blustery week in June. He had never before won a tournament. He was only 21. 'The New Gary Player', he was called. And the sceptics who muttered 'Fluke victory' or 'Flash in the pan' were answered inside three weeks when Cobie tied with Roberto de Vicenzo for the French Open. That was in 1964. A new personality in tournament golf had arrived all right and what an admirable feet-on-the-ground outlook Cobie possessed about it all.

Cobie has gone on winning round the world ever since. But fame was still fresh when he looked back on the achievements of that first big summer in Britain.

'The thing people remark upon most is the fact that I am so young to have done what I have,' he said. 'What they don't realise is that I have been working at my game for seven years. That is quite a long time.'

The truth of this observation gathers impact as you learn

just what Cobie has put into those seven years, the thought, the drive, the sheer hard, slogging work.

Despite his great leap forward Legrange went on to say: 'I am still a hundred miles from what I want to do. Look at Nicklaus and Palmer, the way they seem to win when the prizes are greatest. Here am I, winning the Masters and failing to qualify in the Open. I tie for the French Open and straight away fail in Ireland. I must be able to go when I say "Go". I have still to discover what is lacking. Is it in my swing, or in my thinking? I'm fishing, I'm working, I'm learning all the time. I'll find out.'

After winning the Masters Legrange said his success came from a year of hard work rebuilding his swing, and from better thinking. *The Power of Positive Thinking*, a book by Dr. Vincent Peal published in America, was among the many he read to achieve mental mastery of the game.

Cobie's thinking, positive and clear, comes through to you at any meeting with him. He has a direct and simple way of expressing himself. He tackles the multi-problems of tournament golf in the same way, cutting them down to basics and tackling them with a singleminded determination reminiscent of Ben Hogan and Gary Player, two giants of the game who have both had a direct influence on Cobie's golfing career.

I asked the fair-haired young Master golfer to go right back to the beginnings. He was born at Boksburg, Transvaal, on October 22nd, 1942, has two sisters, both his junior. His father, a former mine captain and now a store owner at Margate, near Durban, is a golf addict of long standing, once as low as two-handicap, now six. Cobie's mother plays too. His earliest recollections of the game are at the age of nine when his father's work took him to Shabani in Southern Rhodesia as manager of an asbestos mine. Legrange senior was then so keen that in the absence of a golf course he improvised one in order to keep his game going.

'I remember him cutting rough fairways out of the veldt and bush and I'd go along to watch him practise,' Cobie recalls. 'But it was not until I was 14 that I took any interest in the game and then it was almost an accident, a combination of circumstances. I was very keen on soccer at school but a torn ligament in my left knee put me out of the game abruptly.

'About that time Father bought himself a set of new clubs and handed his old ones on to me. We were now settled in Margate and I began go play at the Golf and Country Club, a shortish resort course which could flatter your golf, but fairly tight and calling for accuracy. That's why I have always put emphasis on keeping 'em straight, I suppose. When the rest of the school was playing football I would cycle the two miles to the course to play golf. First it was three times a week. Then four. Then five. Finally I used to bunk school to get on the golf course.'

That is how Cobie got the bug.

'Father said I had got to make up my mind whether it was to be school or golf,' he continued. 'I told him I was not the studious type. I just wanted to play golf. I wanted to become a professional. So he took me away from school when I was 15. That is when I really began to work at the game. We decided that I would give it a go for two years to see what progress I could make before actually taking the plunge into the game as a pro.'

So began the career of Cobie Legrange, tournament professional. For two solid years he went to the club each day at eight in the morning and left at six at night, taking just a short break for lunch. For more than 700 days he served his apprenticeship just hitting golf shots. The generous climate of the Natal coast was on his side. Rain was all that would drive him indoors, and the wet days could be counted on one hand almost. Caddies to pick up balls were cheap. What a contrast it provides to the entry of a youngster into the game in Britain.

When 15 Cobie ventured into the Natal Amateur Championship. He was beaten heavily in the third round. Back he went to his practice. There was still a long way to go. 'I would play on Wednesday, Saturday and Sunday afternoons. The rest of the time I spent on the practice tee or putting green and worked at hitting shots,' Cobie said.

On what lines did he build his game, was he professionally taught? Back home at Margate, Cobie possesses a well-thumbed copy of Hogan's *Modern Fundamentals of Golf*. Throughout the book certain passages are underlined for emphasis. The tutor who selected these passages for their extra importance was none but Gary Player.

'Gary's father and mine knew each other because both were in the mining industry,' Cobie explains. 'Mr. Player was at our house one day when he offered to arrange a meeting with Gary. I was then 16. That is when we went through Hogan's book together and Gary emphasised certain points. I also took every opportunity of watching good players when they came our way—Gary, Harold Henning, Trevor Wilkes, Tommy Bolt, Dai Rees and Ken Bousfield. I studied them on cine shots I took. I also had cine films made of my own swing. I have spent hours watching films of Palmer, Nicklaus and other leading Americans.'

A milestone in Cobie's life came not long after his seventeenth birthday. He finished runner-up in the South African Amateur championship, beaten three and two by Murray Grindrod, the Cambridge Blue.

'Father said to me one day he would give me the money

to go to Cape Town and play in the South African Amateur. It meant travelling 2,000 miles. I said to him, "Don't pull the wool over my eyes. I am not ready for that." He insisted. I went. I beat Bob Williams, a Springbok [South African international], John da Costa, a former pro; and, in the semi-final, Dave Symons, a Springbok who has since won the title. Losing at the last hurdle was disappointing. It made me realise that I had still a lot to learn.'

That was in 1960, the year Cobie turned professional. He continued his dedicated apprenticeship, mixing the practice with tournament forays whenever he could. In the spring of 1962 he was one of the annual flock of young South Africans to make the migratory passage to Britain and the Continent. For 19-year-old Cobie it was a somewhat chastening experience.

Experience, though, was not all he took back to Margate. There was also the resolve that he had to make a radical change in his swing. Out of that change came the swing that won the Masters.

In Cobie's own words: 'When I came over in 1962 I knew I had a loop in my swing. I took the club away outside and looped it inside before coming down. I thought that was my style, that I could play with what I had. British conditions taught me different. In your winds I could not get by with the "soft" hit this swing gave. The loop caused loss of power, lack of zip at impact. A season here showed me there was something radically wrong. That I would have to look a bit harder. I went home knowing that I really had to work this thing out.'

Legrange worked on his problem for the whole of 1963. He did not come to Europe. He spent over 300 days on the practice ground. This is what he did: 'I started to swing a little flatter. I cut out the loop. It was all so completely different that at first I could not even hit the ball. I was coming to it six inches behind. But I worked something out—a flatter swing, with more firmness at the top. It gave me the clubhead speed at impact I needed.'

That, then, is the origin and construction of Cobie's winning swing. But he is quick to point out that a good swing is only part of the complete golfer. Two things rank with the swing—thinking and fitness. He has no fads of diet, but does not smoke or drink alcohol. Back at home he built his golf muscles training three times a week under local physical-culture expert John Mitchell. Cobie, 170 lb. and 5 ft. 10½ in., says: 'I want to make the most of the physique I have. Maybe I have small hands, but I want them to be as strong as they can be.'

The single-minded young South African went home from Britain in 1962 also with the resolve to improve his thinking on the game as well as his technique. How well he succeeded his subsequent achievements show.

'The majority of players hit the ball well. The person who thinks best is the one who succeeds,' this young man with an old head says. 'This game can catch you at any time. You must learn to have control over your body. I have read all the books I could lay my hands on to improve my mental approach to the game. They all come back to one thing: Having faith in yourself.'

The greatest test of Cobie's faith in himself came in the last five holes of the 1964 Dunlop Masters when a five-shot lead over the field began to dwindle away without him hitting a really bad shot. I asked him how he felt about the run of six, five, six—one over par at each of 14, 15 and 16. How did it affect him? He said: 'I was not nervous. I told myself, "It's no use getting excited. If it's your turn to win you'll win." I knew I wanted a three and a five at the last two holes. Once I had hit that good three-iron to the 17th green I knew I was home.'

That Masters brought a new dimension to Cobie's golf

career—fame. There were autograph hunters, backslaps, interviews, and big galleries. He rides it all with calmness and with grace. 'I did not expect to win a tournament this year. Lots of placings in the first 10, that's what I hoped for this year,' Cobie admitted. His title and the big prize that went with it were the preface to campaigning in America. Once more a young invader has set a pace young British professionals seem rarely able to match.

Cobie offers the explanation: 'Your conditions are against early progress. Compare your climate with South Africa's. The weather is so unpredictable here, so severe in the winter. There is no incentive to a regular practice programme. Playing in some of your wind and rain could do your swing more harm than good. Your caddies are so much more expensive than the boys we have in South Africa.

'But I do think that young British pros should go to the Continent more. You can improve your golf by playing in the Continental tournaments. They are on good courses, the climate is more favourable. You can play and then rely upon the weather for two hours or so on the practice ground every day.'

Here is one more example of the positive thinking that puts Cobie Legrange where he is—on the way to the top. For though this talented and dedicated young man won Britain's Masters title, there was no hint of complacency or resting on laurels. Think back on what he said: '. . . I am still a hundred miles from what I want to do.' Listen to his explanation for the unremitting effort he has put into the game: 'Whatever I do I want to do properly. The game of golf is very hard to master. I made up my mind I would not let it beat me. The only way was work and more work. But it is still sitting on my head and pushing me down.'

Watching, listening to, and reflecting upon the iron

determination of Cobie Legrange convinces me it will not be long before he will be ripe for his own high standard and 'be able to go when I say "Go" '. Then what a golfer he will be.

Neil Coles

ONE of the highest compliments to a British golfer in recent years was paid to Neil Coles at the 1962 Open championship. It came from Arnold Palmer. When Palmer, eventually the magnificent winner of a sensational championship, checked in at Troon's Marine Hotel one of the first things he did was to ask my golf-writing colleague John Ingham: 'Is Neil Coles playing in the championship?' John, relating the incident later, said there was obvious concern in the great man's enquiry. Equally plain was his relief when told that illness had made Coles a non-starter.

Now Palmer is without peer as a sporting ambassador for the United States. He is tactful, he is the essence of friendliness once he drops a golf club from his mighty fist. But none of these factors coloured his coldly professional query about Coles. Palmer ranked him as a genuine contender for the Open. And how many British golfers could you put in this category over the past dozen years?—Or, should I say, how few?

Palmer's respect for Coles' ability came from first-hand observation. Only in the previous season had Neil shaken off the long-held tag of 'promising young assistant' and really taken his place among the Top Ten of British golf. Palmer was present to see two links in the chain of progress —Neil finishing joint third in Palmer's first British Open at gale-swept Royal Birkdale; and later in the year making an impressive Ryder Cup début at Royal Lytham.

All American golf, not just Palmer, learned that 'rookie' Coles halved his match with reigning U.S. Open champion Gene Littler and defeated Dow Finsterwald, America's 'Mr. Consistency'. Coles, in fact, had wrapped up his Ryder Cup place by midsummer, but for good measure crowned his breakthrough season with his first major tournament win, the Ballantine event. First prize was £1,500, then a record in British golf. One final fact—Coles cracked the Wentworth West Course record, too, shooting a 65, with the American-size ball. This record still stands.

Neil Coles' splendid 1961, with its honours, its glory, and more than £4,000 winnings, was the end of a 10-year climb by the intelligent, determined, unflamboyant Coles. Such was his talent, his application, that once at the top he had no difficulty in staying there. The only real check was an illness in the summer of 1962 when he had pneumonia. He nevertheless made a rousing comeback in the Senior Service tournament at Dalmahoy. Victory there over an international field improved on his own record as Britain's biggest single prize winner, and he is quietly proud of the fact that he was the first British player to win £2,000 at one go.

The 1963 season, therefore, was Coles' first full one at the top. When it ended he could look back on a trail of triumphs so quietly and unassumingly compiled that the whole year went by without any panegyrics written about him.

Not that this would worry Neil. He is no hunter of glory or publicity. Achievement seems sufficient reward for the soft-spoken fellow who from April to November took in measured, purposeful stride things like winning the Vardon Trophy, adding Canada Cup colours for England to his Ryder Cup badge, tieing for two big ones, the Martini and

Lionel Platts (Pannal). Yorkshireman who gambled on proving he could make good in tournaments—and won a Ryder Cup place

Harold Henning (South Africa). Graduated in Britain and in Europe to success in the tough circuit of the United States

Cobie Legrange (South Africa).
Dedicated young Springbok
inspired by examples of
countrymen Bobby Locke
and Gary Player

Bruce Crampton (Australia).
Five years of work, work,
work preceded the
breakthrough to success in
American tournaments

Tony Fisher (Sudbury). Unofficial ambassador of British golf on the strange and distant fairways of Nigeria

Leslie King (Golf Clinic, Belgravia). Golf consultation at the Harley Street level in a London indoor school

the Daks, and collecting the bigger cheques so regularly that only Bernard Hunt's then British record winnings of £7,209 surpassed Neil's £3,720 earnings.

On the eve of another season as one of Britain's front-rank tournament players I talked to Neil in the comfort of his fine detached house at Walton-on-Thames. This home was the tangible evidence of transition from the days when his father generously supported his tournament ambitions to the tune of a £250-a-year subsidy. Outside the house were further symbols of success—the Coleses were a two-car family.

'This house instead of a bungalow, new car, a bit more comfort in living, that is all the difference it has made really,' said Neil, answering the question, 'What is life like now you are at the top?' 'It has probably made more difference to my wife Ann. Being able to run a second car has made life pleasanter for her, enabled her to get about more. She has things she wants for the home. The boys [Keith, 12, and Gary, 9] go to private school. Then there is the business I bought; another interest and a source of steady income.'

Neil's business venture is a shoe-repair shop in London's western suburbs. It is a line he knows something about because his father has a chain of such businesses. 'One shop is enough to keep me occupied,' said Neil. 'Tournament golf is an up-and-down affair, and a business like mine gives a more stable income.'

Very soon the subject was back to normal—golf. 'Oh, making the breakthrough was much harder than staying at the top,' Coles revealed. 'You have proved something to yourself once you have won a tournament. Once having won you have more confidence about doing it again. Getting in a position to win is the thing then. I enjoy the competition, I like the challenge of tournaments. It is a thing that gets you. You get a bit depressed at times if the scores won't come. But you have to go on. It gets into your blood.

'The hardest thing to keep at top pitch is putting. This goes off at times. To get it back I experiment a bit, perhaps a lighter grip, or concentrating on taking the clubhead back lower. I don't normally switch putters. That is the only part of my game I do experiment with. Everything else is the same as I have developed over the years. I have still never read a golf book or studied theory. My swing is "all my own work" you could say. I want the feeling of having the clubhead square all the way through the swing. To get this I have my own individual address—hooding the clubface.'

As we talked on Neil mentioned one of the minor problems a top tournament professional has to battle with in preparation for a new season. He was trying to find the clubs which suited him from three sets of new Letters model. 'You ask for your well-tried favourites to be copied, but though they may look right the replacements are rarely quite right. So you go on searching for some that feel just right. You have got to be happy with what you play with. This game is so psychological.'

The talk moved on to the Ryder Cup, and Neil said: 'Producing your best golf in that I found harder than doing it in a tournament. I suppose it is the responsibility to others instead of playing just for yourself. There's the crowd, the captain, your team-mates.'

Competition at world level has brought no changes, no modifications to Coles' swing, no changes in technique despite rubbing shoulders with the best players in the world. Does he consider himself a better player now than in the breakthrough season of 1961? 'Experience-wise, yes. But not in striking the ball, that's just the same. You learn all the time from playing tournaments.

'In the Piccadilly at Hillside in 1962 I had a poor last

round which cost several hundred pounds, even a chance of beating Peter Thomson for the £2,000 first prize. The final round was played on Sunday. I had a starting time just after two o'clock. I got to the course at 10.30 or 11. Waiting around all that time I became mentally tired and all twitched-up. The lesson—don't go to the course too early.

'Another rather obvious lesson came home to me in the Carrolls tournament at Woodbrook. Bernard Hunt was running away with it, but there was a battle for second place. I was well in it with 34 to the turn, but apparently put myself right out of it when I started back with a four at the short 10th and a seven at the 11th, through going out of bounds. Then I did the last seven holes 2, 2, 4, 4, 4, 2, 3. An eagle, five birdies and a par. I finished in 66 and beat Kel Nagle by one stroke for second place.

'That taught me more than a bookful of words, "Keep going. Anything can happen in this game." Before that experience I was inclined to give up a bit too easily.'

That the lesson was well learned, Neil proved in the Senior Service shortly after. Following two indifferent rounds, he stormed into third place with 66, 66 on the last day.

Coles has established a reputation as a good pressure player by his performances in the biggest money events. How does he account for it? 'It's just the thought of all that money at the end of it,' he says lightly. 'I don't have any special counteraction when the pressure is on. Nothing beyond giving myself a sharp talking-to about keeping cool, not doing anything silly, and getting on with the job.' He adds: 'When I win I am usually putting pretty well—it takes an average of 28–29 putts a round to win a tournament. In my final 65 in the Ballantine I had 25 putts and a chip-in.'

This is inspiration golf. The kind that not only wins

tournaments but Open championships. Could Coles win an Open? He thinks he could. 'If I got into a position to win with a few holes to play I would not be frightened. But I have only once started well in the Open. It seems to get such a build up. That's why British players find it such a tough tournament. If my peak coincided with the Open I could do well in it.

'No, I can't say I give a special place to preparation for the Open. I tackle the season as a whole. I seem to start slowly, reach a peak about May and June, and then come again at the end of the season.

'I think a British player could win the Open without building up for it on the U.S. circuit. It is the men, not the tournament system over here. We have not had a world-class player since Henry Cotton. Dai Rees has been closest and his record in the Open bears this out. He has been close more often than any other home player.'

Neil Coles has achieved much in golf. His foremost remaining ambition is, naturally, the Open championship. He says: 'There's only the Open and the U.S. circuit in which I have to prove myself. As far as American golfers are concerned I am not overawed by them. Palmer and Nicklaus apart, they aren't supermen. If I played their circuit long enough I could hold my own. When I played the winter circuit for a month in 1962 I felt I could have done well if I had stopped. But I am not keen on the way of living. The American circuit remains a challenge, but how can you think of it without being sponsored. The summer circuit is the one to play—better courses, bigger prizes. But it means an outlay of £2,000 for six months, plus all you might have won at home. Where has the British tournament pro got that kind of money? All right, he makes £5,000, lives at a rate of £2,000 a year, has £1,000 in expenses, pays a hefty chunk of tax, and there is not all that much left.' I see what Neil means.

Another thing that deters him from an American invasion and other international golf is his dislike of flying. He flew regularly until a few years ago, making two trips to America, going to Ireland and the Continent. The aversion began after a flight back from a tournament in Scotland in 1962. 'Not a bad flight, as such. But I got twitched up over it, felt claustrophobic, and can't face the thought of flying again. Just don't like the idea any more. I don't say I won't ever fly again, but I will have to feel a lot different before I do,' Neil says frankly.

Neil's natural athleticism is masked by his thinning hair, quiet manner and complete lack of flamboyance. During schooldays at Letchworth in Hertfordshire he was a crack sprinter and first XI left winger. He has the big but compact build ideal for the golfer. Perhaps the most significant of all his physical gifts is that he is naturally left-handed. He kicks and throws a ball left-handed, plays snooker and darts that way, can play table tennis with either hand, and at cricket bowls left arm and bats right. Left-side control with a golf club comes easily to him. Important, too, is his gift for carpentry, model- and cabinet-making. Neil has constructed his own boats and all kinds of household furniture and fittings. He is gifted with his hands. It goes a long way to explain his superb touch with golf clubs.

Since his breakthrough no year has gone by without Coles consolidating his place as one of the three or four leading players in the British Isles. He passed Bernard Hunt's money record with some £7,800 winnings in 1964, and in 1966 topped £8,000, to improve his own mark. In successive years he won the News of the World Match-Play championship. Internationally he figured in that unforgettable first Piccadilly World Match-Play final, losing narrowly two and one to Palmer; and when the rich Carling World championship came to Britain at Royal Birkdale Coles was the foremost home challenger, finishing third to

Australia's Bruce Devlin and Billy Casper, then American Open champion. He brought his trophy case near completion with the Dunlop Masters title in 1966. He soon may have to build himself another one. At 33—born September 26th, 1934—Neil has a lot of winning golf ahead yet.

13
Lionel Platts

ONE of the success stories of recent seasons in tournament golf is that in which Yorkshireman Lionel Platts made a sudden leap into the £3,000-a-year bracket. The husky Sheffield-born heavyweight made the decision one winter to throw up his club job at Thorndon Park in Essex to play the circuit as a full-time tournament performer. Lionel made a sparkling start to the new phase of his golfing life. Four times he finished second in important tournaments, and in the autumn on the big and rugged Turnberry links he proved master of all the top boys in the Braemar Seven-Club event.

The weight of this achievement can best be measured against the modest efforts of the three or four years immediately before. Platts won both major assistants' tournaments in 1961, but was never more than on the fringe of the Top 20 among the seniors. Even in his best season he had not earned a place among the four-figure earners in the official P.G.A. money list.

The transition is startling. Is it just a simple case of ceasing to be a club pro and becoming a tournament specialist? This helped, but it is very far from being the whole story. This strong and solid citizen Platts has had to work his way to the top the hard way. No short cuts, no leg-ups, no sponsors. Just plain, honest graft. What you would expect in fact from a quiet but tough Yorkshireman.

'I have never had it easy. I have been pretty hard up as an assistant. But I don't mind that. I think it is better for you. I don't believe in sponsors and making things easy,' said candid Platts.

Lionel explained his surge into the Top 10 by the effect of his decision to become a tournament professional. 'Now, if I don't play well I don't earn a living. Before, my thinking and my attitude was always influenced by having an income from the club job to fall back on. My incentive is greater. It has to be with a wife and three young children.' Lionel met his wife Beryl when a young assistant with Frank Jowle at Edgbaston, Birmingham.

How did he come to take the plunge, to make the considerable gamble on his playing ability? 'I wanted to give myself a chance in the tournaments. For the previous four years I had always made my expenses, and that means making £1,000 to play the British circuit for a season. I knew I could play well enough. And it is no good trying the circuit for a living unless you can. You've got to be able to play,' Lionel emphasised—meaning that one's game has to be fully equipped with all the shots and adequate power. 'You can't get by on just chipping and putting if you want a permanent living from the tournaments alone.'

Here's evidence of a streak of Yorkshire hard-headedness, a willingness to face the stark facts of tournament playing.

To choose tournament golf as a way of life requires not just the physique and talent for the game. Many have had these qualities and failed to make the grade. A lot of character is required too. Tenacity, ambition, patience. Nerve, will-to-win, and, slowest of all to acquire, experience. All these make up your tournament winner. Platts has them. He has spent half his life getting somewhere close to what he wants, more than that time dreaming about it.

Lionel was born in Sheffield on October 10th, 1934. His father was a male nurse who played a bit of golf at Hillsborough. Lionel caddied there and became a junior member, handicap two. He wanted a job as assistant at the club with Jack Shanks, but there was no opening at the time he left school. So at 15 he was sent by Shanks to Frank Jowle at Lees Hall, and stayed till he went into the Army three years later.

Said Platts: 'I learnt a lot from Frank. He is the man who helped me most to get a sound swing and knowledge of the game in all its branches. In those days I got 30 bob a week wages and had 300 sets of clubs and 200 pairs of shoes to clean every week on Monday and Tuesday.'

It was not the drudgery of being an assistant that made Platts dream about being a tournament player. He says: 'I began to swing a golf club as soon as I could walk and my ambition has always been to become a tournament pro. I have always been keen on sport. I played for Sheffield United "A" team at outside-left. But as a youngster I always wanted to play golf, not become a club pro. My thoughts have always come back to that. It has always been at the back of my mind.'

That Lionel has eventually got there is evidence of that essential tenacity and patience, qualities that will always stand you in good stead in golf, the most frustrating of all games.

Platts went into the Royal Signals, got a posting to Germany, and a surprising amount of golf. He was stationed near Hamburg, managed to obtain a considerable amount of play on the Falkenstein course, and there won the British Army of the Rhine championship, beating fellow Northerner Tony Coop in the process. He was good enough at 19 to finish in the first 20 of the German Open won by Bobby Locke after the historic double play-off with Dai Rees. That was in 1954.

I

After the Army he renewed his association with Frank Jowle, who had meanwhile moved to Edgbaston. After some 15 months came the move to Selsdon Park as one of Harry Weetman's assistants.

'I left Frank Jowle for no other reason than wanting more scope and opportunity which I thought I would get around London,' Platts said.

Lionel rapidly built the reputation of being a power hitter, right in the class of his spectacular boss Weetman. He made his first bid to break through among the star assistants at the 1957 Gor-Ray championship. Lionel led for much of the way, was finally pipped by the deadly short game of Scot George Low, then at his best.

The same year he made the move to Thorndon Park and at once increased his opportunities for tournament play under the now-retired Sid Dennis.

It was an arduous apprenticeship, chiselling out precious experience with no great financial return. The most promising showing was to finish joint fifth in the 1959 P.G.A. championship, won by Dai Rees in his native Wales, at Ashburnham. Up another notch or two in 1960—close-up at the Coombe Hill and Hartsbourne assistants' classics, and even more significant, qualifying for the Dunlop Masters for the first time. Another pointer to the future came with a share of the lead on the Burma Road when the Dunlop tournament was last staged at Wentworth.

There was still a lot of learning to be done. A considerable challenge was met in 1961. Lionel knew it was his last chance in the two big assistants' tournaments. He was booked to take over from Sid Dennis at Thorndon at the end of the tournament season. He was expected to win each time. To his credit he pulled off this double despite being the topweight favourite. The years 1962 and 1963 were ordinary. The club job was a preoccupation. His tournament career virtually stood still. His one break-out was to win the Sunningdale Foursomes with his boon companion David Snell, as backmarkers and against all the odds, leaving a trail of distinguished victims in their wake. So the experience was slowly filed away.

You don't, however, suddenly start winning big money because you have been playing a long time. That's just one thing. The talent is another. And then there is the nerve and the temperament to be able to play when the stakes are really big. You could be born with this gift. You might acquire it. Lionel did—in a tough school. He was known around Essex as a formidable money player with sporting amateurs who want a big gamble. In his own field another Arthur Lees, the big-betting maestro of Sunningdale, oddly enough another Sheffielder.

Says Lionel: 'I do play privately for quite a lot of money. Both in singles and four-balls. Of course you can write about it. I don't mind who knows. A £100 is a normal stake on an 18-hole match. At times it gets considerably more. I don't like it to get any bigger than £100, but you have to. Chaps want a chance to win money back. So what can you say? I don't like being beaten. I have never thrown a match in my life. I have made a lot of money this way.

'Sure, it helps your mental attitude in tournaments. That's what makes your golf. I have had as much as £500 of my own money on the last hole of a match. That is bound to toughen you for the chance of winning a sum like it in the last few holes of a tournament. I learned to play hard for money when I was a boy at Lees Hall. Six- or seven-balls between myself and members for a ten-bob sweep were an everyday thing. That is how I used to live.'

This reveals how the mind of a tournament player can be built. How about the method of Lionel Platts? Is he still a slammer in the Weetman mould, with all the destructive shots and spectacular recoveries of crowd-pleasing

Harry? That may have once been the case, but not any more. Says Lionel: 'I am not so long as I used to be. I have steadied down at the expense of length. I play to keep the ball on the fairway, to hit the safe shot all the time. My long game gives me no trouble. If anything does go wrong it is in my short game.'

Lionel normally uses a mallet putter, with a tap action. He is a sensible rather than slave-like practiser. 'I never do too much at a time on the practice ground. An average session would be two hours hitting shots, and a half hour chipping and putting.'

Reg Knight, the Wanstead professional and keen observer of the golf swing, has long been a friend and confidant of Lionel's. Reg was instrumental in Platts carrying the Wanstead flag so prominently in 1964 as the club's tournament pro. Knight has played a lot of golf with Platts and sees his method like this:

'It is very American, perhaps the most Americanised swing in British golf. It is a straightforward, no-frills swing keeping the blade absolutely square through the ball and after impact. Lionel has built it himself with constant practice and play. He has put in a lot of work in the winters. You have to be very strong to play that way. Not much wrist work, more arms and body. Not many could play liked Lionel. He has sacrificed a bit of length but gets that back in consistency and accuracy.'

Platts's method certainly took to the big ball like a duck to water. 'It was a pity to go back to the small ball from my point of view,' he says. 'I did not think I would like the big ball but I find it helped the short game a lot. I found I hit my iron shots higher. I get a very low flight with the small ball.'

Lionel has had a winter tour of South Africa and had his first look at America in a Carling World championship. He observes: 'The course they said was so tough was not much different to the park courses we play on. A bit longer, that's all. It suited me all right. The American tournament pros all hit the ball a long way. There must be at least 100 good players over there. I'd love to go on their circuit but it's too expensive.'

Determined Lionel made the Ryder Cup team in 1965. It took time but he has made the first bridgehead of his boyhood dreams. He really is someone in the world of tournament golf. This striking individualist, often to be found seeking the lone relaxation of an angler, sees 10 years of tournament golf ahead of him, though he has now taken out the insurance of a club job at Pannal, back in his native county.

Part of my talk with Lionel was on a fishing expedition. They were not rising particularly well on a chill autumn day. In two hours the catch was one half-pounder. I left him to it. Lionel came in at dusk—with a catch of four. The patient, tenacious Yorkshireman even at play!

'Fishing is the finest possible relaxation from tournaments,' he says. 'When my eyes are on that float there is not another thought in my head. Too many players make the mistake of hanging around the clubhouse on a diet of golf, golf, golf. I believe in getting away from it when the day's work is done.'

Lionel's final thoughts on this breakthrough were: 'I don't think it would have happened if I had not taken the chance of leaving the club to play only in tournaments. I knew I had got to make money. That was the spur. I only wish I had done it sooner, though perhaps there were not the opportunities a few years ago there are now. Winning comes when you get the breaks. Many get into a position to win. I did in the Schweppes and the Blaxnit before I won the Braemar. Everyone hits a bad shot in a round of golf. If you get a break at the right time it need not be fatal.'

Lionel Platts, it seems, timed his break-in to the big

time to perfection. Events proved Reg Knight right in saying, 'Anyone who plays as well as Lionel had no business being tied up with a club job.' Singleminded and serious, tough and talented, Lionel Platts made his biggest gamble to date pay off.

14

Bruce Crampton

BRUCE CRAMPTON, citizen of Sydney, Australia, was able to boast when he was 28 years old that he had had only 26 birthdays. The explanation has nothing to do with Leap Year. It is that twice in recent years Bruce has lost a day of his young life in crossing the International Dateline when flying out of San Francisco to Australia. Crampton, a handsome and husky fellow of 185 lb. and close to six feet, got quite a kick over telling me this piquant fact about himself.

Its significance is that here is an Australian who has chosen to become one of the globe-trotting international brigade of golf. Up to 38 weeks of his year are spent on the grinding tournament circuit of the United States, which Bruce rightly calls 'the toughest golf school in the world'. He has been going there since 1957. Since 1962 his winnings have comfortably passed the £10,000-a-year mark, and his performances in the States gained the recognition of a place in Australia's Canada Cup side. Only Norman Von Nida, Peter Thomson, Kel Nagle and Bruce Devlin, among Aussies of the modern era, have achieved more in tournament golf than Crampton.

He owes part of his success to one of Australia's trailblazers. Bruce says: 'Norman von Nida has been a wonderful help to me ever since my days as a kid amateur.

He played with me for three or four years and before I was twenty I had learned all the experience it had taken Norman a lifetime to acquire. Since I have begun to make money in golf, Norman has extended his advice to all my affairs. We are in fact partners in business, owning factories which we rent to manufacturing firms.'

It is true that von Nida launched Crampton into the rugged but rewarding field of big golf. I remember Bruce coming with Frank Phillips under the wing of 'The Von' to make his début in England at Moor Park in 1956. Bruce went back to become Australian Open champion at the age of 20.

He paid return visits to Britain without uprooting any trees. He gained more prominence in fact for voicing his opinions of the stuffy attitude and the atmosphere encountered at a certain Scottish club which took an unrepeated date on the tournament calendar.

Bruce says now: 'I was the centre of a little strife back there in Scotland. It is because I am honest. I speak of things as I find them and don't believe it is right to be a hypocrite.' This is a typically Australian attitude, of course, and one which gleams right through Crampton's outlook on life and golf.

From von Nida came the initial encouragement. But it is Bruce's character, cold tenacity and skill which have made him a success in that tough American school. It is this Crampton I want to present as the example of the only way to the top rank in world-class golf. This story is a classic lesson to all young players who dream of being Hogans or Palmers.

Crampton says: 'I have been to the States every year since I was first invited to the Masters in 1957. On that trip I won money for the first time in the Houston Open—$800. But it was mainly for a look-see. I went to learn something. In 1958 I went again. I learned some more and went home to work on it some more. There was a lot to learn and a lot to work on.

'If you are to make progress in the U.S. there are certain processes you have to go through. The first is pre-qualifying, a fierce survival of the fittest. The same thing goes on in the main tournament, where you have to learn to make the cut. The art of this is the ability to sum up courses and how best to play them. The next stage is getting in the money. After that it's the climb to the big cheques. Finally there is the business of winning.'

Bruce had to wait till 1961, his fifth year on the U.S. tour, before his first win—in the Milwaukee Open. 'Winning demands much more than getting into the money, it's something totally different,' he continued. 'You have to play yourself into a position to win. At Milwaukee I led after three rounds. I had built up confidence by getting into the top ten in tournaments. This time the breaks went my way.'

Golf in America, Crampton points out, is technically quite a different game to that played in the small-ball (1·62 in.) countries. 'After my visit to America in 1957 I began to work on radical changes in my game. With the American ball, their fairways and watered greens, it is a matter of flying the ball through the air and pitching it in soft. There's no pitch and run shot. Flags are hidden behind traps. You have to use the all air route. All this meant a change in my grip and stance, and in the striking of the ball. With the big ball you have to hit less down on it than the small ball. You nip it off the grass and take shallower divots—unlike the way Harry Weetman or Dave Thomas hit their shots.'

Crampton's 'arrival' on the U.S. circuit was a gradual process—in 1961 a tournament winner but only 57th on that revealing yardstick of success, the U.S.P.G.A.'s list of official winnings. The next year he shot to ninth and topped $31,000; in 1963, $32,000; 1964, $19,000; 1965, $56,000; 1966, $22,500.

Bruce learned, he says: '. . . Mainly by observation, though I had good advice from two regulars of the tour, Jack Fleck and Bob Toski.' Crampton is teetotal and a non-smoker, extremely fit and very strong. When he went to U.S. for the winter tour in 1962 he staggered even the Americans by a record non-stop run of 38 tournaments from January through to September. The 'Iron Man' became his tag.

Bruce says: 'Good food and the right amount of rest are all I worry about. No exercises beyond the actual playing of golf.' He considers his success in the last two years mainly a matter of time-serving and experience. 'I have been able to think about playing the course and the shots, instead of how I am swinging the club,' he explains. With all his substantial achievements behind him, he still strives to climb further up the ladder. His sights are now on America's three major events of the calendar—the Masters, Open and P.G.A. championships. He has done well in all of them, and made the pace in the 1963 P.G.A. until overhauled by the fantastic Jack Nicklaus in the final round.

Crampton's great asset is a wonderful putting stroke, regarded by Gary Player as one of the three best he has known—'Bruce Crampton ranks with Bobby Locke and Arnold Palmer as the greatest putters I know, and Bruce's actual stroke is the best action of them all,' Gary says.

Candid Crampton admits there are two things he has to work on to continue his ascent in his chosen profession. 'My driving has to be straighter and I am working on that. The other thing is myself, my attitude. Temperament I guess you call it. I am inclined to get hot. I am working on that too.'

Bruce and I met up again at the 1963 Canada Cup in Paris. It was the first time for five years, when he last played the British and Continental circuit, and made his last appearance in the British Open at Royal Lytham. 'Don't get me wrong about the British Open. I would dearly like to win it, but in recent years I have not been ready to make a real bid,' he says. 'Coming to play in it just for prestige would cost too much money. It would mean missing at least two big tournaments.'

He says frankly why he has chosen to concentrate on the American circuit. 'In America you have the world's best players, the biggest money and I like the life there. The weather is generally warm and settled and you play in the light clothes I am used to playing in at home. This kind of spoils you for anywhere else. Then in America the professional golfer is admired and respected and they are powerful enough as a body to run the tournaments by professionals for professionals, a state of affairs you don't get in other countries.'

Bruce continued: 'The emphasis is on skill on the U.S. tournament circuit, with luck eliminated as far as possible.'

Crampton is a supporter of the American way of golf even to the extent of saying that a universal-sized ball is desirable and it should be the bigger ball. 'It is harder to hit straight, but that would produce better strikers,' he says. But he remains proud to be an Australian, glad of the chance to represent his country in the international Canada Cup. He is an advocate of a wider field of selection for the Ryder Cup. 'It is so one-sided in the States that there is little interest by the public over there. The Commonwealth should combine with Britain to give America real opposition. I am sure such an event would have great support if taken to Australia or New Zealand.'

I asked Bruce for a final word of advice and encouragement to the ambitious British tournament player, based upon his long experience in America. He said: 'To me going to America is the only way to improve. It is the toughest competitive golf in the world. You have to be prepared to spend $250 a week. And it is no use expecting to make a quick killing—the opposition is too strong, too tough, too rugged for that. You have to be prepared for knock-downs and to make drastic changes in your game. Most of all there has to be a change of attitude—you have to treat tournament golf as a business, something that demands all your thought and attention.'

There is no doubt that this single-minded and forthright young man Bruce Crampton follows every one of his own precepts. All that's left to say is—and look where it has got him!

15

Leslie King

'MY pupils range from Indian princes to taxi-drivers. In between come ambassadors, peers of the realm, wealthy men of commerce and of industry—and their wives—amateurs of Walker Cup standing, and fellow golf pros young and old.'

The speaker was Leslie King. He runs London's most sophisticated and heavily patronised indoor school. His words were not boastful. There was no need for that. The deeds speak much louder.

There is his address for a start—in Lowndes Square, Knightsbridge, in the squash court of a block of select apartments. King admits freely that 20th is the highest place he ever occupied in a tournament, but no Ryder Cup player can demand a higher lesson fee. If you telephoned BELgravia 2468 to book one of his strictly rationed half-hours the odds are that it would be two to four weeks before you would receive an appointment.

This is a golf consultation at the Harley Street level. King gave Sean Connery the swing that beat Goldfinger. His casebook includes, too, national amateur champions, male and female, two P.G.A. Close champions, overseas tournament stars, and countless fellow professionals who have gone away to spread this gospel of better teaching at their clubs.

The school is in its fifteenth year. Its success did not just happen. The foundations were laid in King's prior service as a club professional for more than 30 years. The vital ingredients of King's teaching are his knowledge and interpretation of the golf swing, his personality and skill in putting it over, a high sense of duty to every pupil that comes to him, and an unflagging enthusiasm. Plus the fact that he teaches a *method*. Leslie scorns the creed of those who claim to mould a swing to fit the pupil. . . . 'These teachers must have memories like a card index file,' he scoffs. 'If you teach a set method all you have to remember is the progress each pupil has made.'

The method did not just happen either. Its evolution is the most fascinating part of the Leslie King story. It goes back to his earliest days in the golf game. Leslie was born at New Malden, Surrey, the son of an estate bailiff. He was introduced to golf through his father's friendship with one of British golf's immortals, Sandy Herd, man of one Open championship, a palm or baseball grip, and of innumerable waggles. Herd was then at Coombe Hill, one of a trinity of courses, with Coombe Wood and Malden, on the estate which was King senior's domain. Leslie as a lad carried clubs at Coombe Hill, was a fascinated hanger-on at Herd's shop. In time he got a week-end job at the nearby Coombe Wood pro's shop. When he left school he made it a full-time job. . . . 'But I still only got ten bob a week,' he recalls.

Leslie was still in the impressionable teens as an assistant when the incident which was to set the pattern of his golfing life occurred. In the one good suit he possessed and armed with a drainpipe bag filled with five irons, three assorted woods, and a putter, he took himself to Wentworth to match his swing with the current masters. The venture was as near a disaster as any hopeful tournament tyro could expect to encounter. It poured with rain. His best suit was ruined. Worse, his morning round totalled 99. Then came the crowning misery. As he stood at the score-board the massive figure of one of golf's contemporary giants, pipe-smoking Ted Ray, loomed up into Leslie's consciousness with the chortled comment, 'Ho, ho! Who's is this cricket score?' It could only have belonged to King, L. (Coombe Wood asst.).

'Those words of Ted Ray stuck into me like a knife. They really got up my back. I went home with my tail truly between my legs,' Leslie recalled.

To complete the searing misery, King in his sopping wet suit, laboriously made a four-stage journey home by means of a walk to Virginia Water station, two changes of train, and a bus ride. This was long before the days of to-every-young-assistant-his-own-motor-car. The dismal youth that night considered his career in golf was in ruins. Next morning he went to his boss at Coombe Wood and gave in his notice.

Before the week expired his employer asked him whether he had secured another job. Leslie had not. Whereupon he received the then princely offer of staying on at 30s. a week—three times his old wage—plus a junior assistant under him, and a half-day off every week. Leslie was hooked. He felt wanted again. He was saved for golf.

On he went at his job. But those words of Ted Ray still rankled. Something had to be done about it. He saved diligently and acquired an old belt-drive Douglas motor-bike and he began to put his half-days to use watching all the good golf he could. Money matches, exhibitions, what tournaments there were. Under his enquiring eye came the giants of his day—Herd, George Duncan, Abe Mitchell, J. H. Taylor.

'The idea of learning about the golf swing for teaching was the farthest thing from my mind. It was my game that I was interested in. I wanted to show I could do well in tournaments. That's what drove me on. The method I built up from my observations was meant for me. Passing it on to others was just an accident, a by-product,' Leslie explained.

'The first thing I did was to discard my imitation of Sandy Herd's palm grip. Nearly all the rest used the Vardon grip. Then I worked on the position of my finish. I noticed that the best players kept the club high up beside the head; they did not take it round their body and swing round themselves. I began to give some kind of decent shape to my swing. Abe Mitchell with his short finish, and Sandy Herd despite his grip, had a similar sort of backswing to J. H. Taylor—a lovely shoulder turn and balance was common to all of them. So different to the way I used to hack the club up, sway from my hips, drop the left shoulder and wobble around. I was going around like this on that old bike until about 1928, before the penny really dropped for me as I was following Abe Mitchell at Coombe Hill one day. I noticed the flex of his right knee as he addressed the ball. That was the real start of making a golf swing for me.

'At that time everyone was saying "brace your right side", or "brace your left side"—instruction which caused a ducked left shoulder movement on the backswing, and a ducked right shoulder on the downswing. For me this leg flex at the address position completely scrubbed out that "braced side" dogma. This was the key to the body poise that is so necessary to a good golf swing. I like to think I was the first professional in the country to put this point over to my fellow pros.

'After that, about 1930, I asked myself, "How can I make a swing for people without giving them a golf club?" I wanted to give my members something to work on when they were not on a golf course. I worked out my exercise for employing upper arm leverage, the freedom of the left arm from the body. This was based upon the realisation that the only reason for winding your shoulders back was to give the upper arm its leverage. Thus, with my earlier discovery of the well-poised finish common among all the great players, I had this back end and the front end of the swing. I had got the parts that would fit together and give the swing a *shape*.

'Hands—I give Henry Cotton his due—are important to the golf swing. You must have hand control. But I think Cotton has got his priorities wrong. Without a good body poise you cannot get the best out of your hands. I put a good overall movement, good position and clubline first. If any of these are faulty then the work the hands do must suffer.'

King continued: 'In my early days of teaching I used to get players down to 5, 8, 12 handicap, but I could not get them any better. Only the odd one got down to scratch. Then one day it dawned on me that an important part was missing. All I had in my mind was shape, shape, shape. I taught my two ends of the swing, but what I hadn't got was a delivery of the club to the ball between those two ends. I had not given it any thought, because it was a part of the swing I had had no difficulty over. I had picked it up by imitation. So there I was sort of turning out, as it were, beautifully bodied motor cars with nothing underneath the bonnet. Once I had got to work on this I was able to turn nice-looking golfers into complete golfers.

'Teaching the delivery is the hardest job of all, because you can put a person into position for every part of the swing, but you cannot make the strike at the ball for them. This is something that has to be done by imitation and feel. Some will do it better than others, naturally. The ideal I aim at is for the delivery to become subconscious. Only then can you stop the interference of a reflex urge to think about hitting the ball. Your mind just won't take two lines of thought at the same time.'

When a newcomer makes his way to King's well-lit net

with its impressive curtain of green canvas at the receiving end, he will start golf 'backwards'. King, after the normal check or instruction in the grip, stance and address (with knees flexed, of course), will start on putting over the front end or finish of the swing. The emphasis would be on poise and balance and taking the club through the impact area to a high finish.

Next would come the shaping of the backswing by the introduction of a valuable home exercise in which the left wrist is grasped by the right hand and the 90-degree turn of the shoulders is accomplished by the movement of the left arm—King's 'upper-left-arm leverage', and his way of building in the left arm's control of the path of the swing. The two movements are then blended together. The swing is taking its shape.

The delivery of club to ball comes next, with accompanying training exercises. Many of the teaching tee's old catch-phrases are savagely tossed aside. But the pupil is left with something to cling to—movements and exercises less difficult to master than a dance routine or a gymnastic drill. King knows what he wants to put over. And it is the same in principle to everyone.

His manner can be forceful and it can be cajoling. King is a commanding and heavily built man and sometimes uses the sergeant-major approach. He will bully you . . . and in the next breath thank you for doing so well or trying so hard. And always he will listen to the pupil's reaction. 'It's a very poor instructor who does not have time to listen to his material,' says King. 'Though you are putting the ideas across, you must always listen to what the pupil understands by your words. Only then can you find out if the picture in the mind of the pupil coincides with what you want them to feel.'

King's attitude to his job of teaching is perhaps all too rare. His creed is—The pupil's enjoyment comes first, my reputation comes second. He says: 'I never give a lesson that's a patch-up job. You look at your pupil and say to yourself, "It's not just now that matters, I've got to try and ensure that I keep this person enjoying golf in ten years' time." You feel you've done a worthwhile job if you have given someone the pleasure and relaxation that they can get from golf.'

Perhaps one of the secrets of this school's success is Leslie King's uncompromising belief in the value of indoor or net teaching. He says, thumping his desk for emphasis: 'Some people say you can only have a lesson on a golf course. This is so wrong and so untrue. Net or school teaching is so superior for imparting position, because the pupil is not worried about where the ball is going and can give all his concentration to obtaining the positions I want him to. On the course, the business of where the ball is going always overrides the positioning of the limbs or body. Then they go back to the old or wrong positions. They can't help it because *mannerisms die hard!* It is for this reason I succeed in changing swings over so quickly here, because there are no distractions through the flight of the ball.'

Much of Leslie's time is spent waging war against bad golfing mannerisms. The first two or three lessons are the most important of your life, he says, '. . . because the very first time you do anything it makes such a deep impression on you that it becomes ingrained as a mannerism.'

But it is given to only a minute number to start their golf under King. To combat mannerisms Leslie says, 'That is why I devised my method of going through the movements of the swing without a golf club. This gives body poise, teaches one to take the arms back in a perfect arc, while keeping the height constant and maintaining good balance. I suggest doing these exercises as the pupil steps out of bed or the bath in the morning—they would forget to do them once the rest of the day's routine had started—and in this way good habits kill the bad ones.'

I asked Leslie if his method teaching could be applied to people of different ages, strength, physique, and be taught to women as well as men.

'No problem at all,' he replied. 'Especially with a simple method like mine. The only thing you are up against is that there are terrific variations in the bone construction of people. One person may have the ideal build for golf because his bone construction lends itself to better poise, better hand action, better movement all round. People with very square shoulders, short neck, or short arms—they are at a disadvantage. Those who walk on the inside of their feet have an advantage over those who walk on the outside, because the latter is prone to make a bad ankle movement on the backswing and does not find it natural to move on to the inside of the foot as they come into the ball. The summing up is that persons of certain bone construction lend themselves to a better job than others. I still put over the same method to everyone.'

Leslie King's casebook is full of fascinating chapters. There was the immensely wealthy man who came to him almost in tears over his inability to get round a golf course in respectable fashion. He was still in this state despite having spent hundreds of pounds on tuition. 'He offered me a present of £100 if I could do something for him,' said King. 'I told him, "I don't want your present. You pay the same as all the rest." Today he is playing to 18 handicap and can go round the course with anyone. What did I do? I remodelled his swing. I took no notice of what he was doing wrong. I just scrubbed the lot and let the right way take over. If I dwelt on his faults I would never stop. It is the only way—to make a fresh start; it is no use putting muck with muck. You get nowhere. It only takes a few weeks to remodel a man's swing.'

Another case was that of a professional's son in the mid-teens who had difficulty in breaking a 100 despite all his father tried to do for him. 'I told —— "It's not the boy's fault, it's you." The father had not got a method. He couldn't give the boy a picture, and without knowing what he was trying to do the boy could not get anywhere. I gave the boy a shaped swing while his father stood here and said, "I'd never thought it possible, what you are doing here!" In a couple of months the boy phoned to say he had broken 80 for the first time. Then he did a 75. He joined his father as an assistant and rapidly built up a teaching clientele.'

King has always been ready to give a helping hand to young professionals and still is despite the failure of many to realise just how much he has done for them. He launched a whole new school of bright young men into the tournaments and good club jobs through the famous clinic for young pros he ran at Malden for over two years.

'I started it because I felt sorry for the young men who were coming back to golf after the war,' King said. 'I remembered my own struggles—having to grope for any knowledge of the game—and felt something should be done. I gave them one day a fortnight. Several went on to win tournaments. Some could have gone further but could not be bothered. They got good club jobs and then sat back.

'I remember a shocking argument with Dick Burton, the 1939 Open champion, over my clinic. He said they were all too old—28 to 30—for me to make golfers out of them, and we were at it hammer and tongs over my method and his idea of the golf swing.

'Six months later Dick came to me, and I shall always admire him for this, completely retracting his words. "I'd never have believed what you have done for these fellows was possible," Dick said. "I've played with one or two in tournaments and the change in their swings is remarkable. If they got the tournament atmosphere now they could go places." Before the clinic ended pros were coming to me from all over the country.'

In 1930 King added a couple of years to his age and landed the job as pro at Merton Park—a Surrey course long since swallowed in London's suburbs. He got the job because of his knowledge of teaching. After the war he moved to Malden where he served until he opened his indoor school in 1954. 'I came up to London thinking I'd have to advertise and canvass all the hotels, but I've never had to do either. Even though I had no telephone for the first three months things went with a bang from the word go. People called personally to book lessons and inside a fortnight I was working to my limit.'

In such a lifetime of teaching, thousands must have come under Leslie's perceptive eye, so I had to ask him, What is the most common fault in golf? 'Swinging round the ball. Caused by bad body poise. How many people look like golfers even before they've taken the club from the ball? How many look nice on the backswing? When you stand on a course and consider this it shakes you. How they are going to bring the clubhead down consistently right, I don't know.

'I am being severe about this, I know, but it worries me. There is no reason why every member of a golf club should be arguing against the other, saying his way is the right way. They should, to my mind, all talk the same language, all be in the same mould.

'Golf is a difficult game, admitted. That is because the hardest thing for the body to do is to repeat something which is a precision movement in which there can be hardly any margin for error.

'In other sports your action is moving, flowing—there isn't the chance for your reflexes to jump you at any moment of the swing with some conflicting thought and so spoil the action. When you are looking at a golf ball you have so much time in comparison with any other ball game.

'But the good thing about golf is that you don't have to be a natural ball or games player to become proficient. International footballers as a class are no better at golf than pen-pushers. Golf can be taught to non-sporting types, people whose reflexes are too slow for tennis, can't throw a dart or wield a billiard cue.

'These people can all become fairly good golfers because it is a game that can be taught more than any other. It is a great leveller—you do not have to be a natural ball player to be a good golfer. I find, in fact, that the non-sportsman is more receptive than the "naturals", who are reluctant to accept teaching and won't get down to the fundamentals. The businessman who takes up golf at 40 is prepared to apply his mind to the game and master the precision movement it demands.'

One of the most studious watchers on the practice ground at an Open championship or a Ryder Cup is Leslie King. He keeps up to date with the modern masters on all golf's great occasions. This is his refresher course.

Five days a week, 48 weeks a year of teaching is an exhausting business mentally. He gets away from golf through motoring and fishing at week-ends to rekindle an enthusiasm which lasts from eight o'clock on Monday morning to 4.30 on the following Friday afternoon. What a character. What a friend to the game of golf and its players. No wonder the world of golf beats a path to Leslie King's door.

16

Tony Fisher

THAT extremely substantial citizen of the golf game, Tony Fisher, is more than just the popular and enthusiastic professional at Sudbury in North-West London. More even than the genial 18 st. Cockney giant who raids the tournament circuit with such gusto and joy of living. Tony's other and lesser-known role is that of British golf's unofficial ambassador to Nigeria, the African republic situated in the steamy tropics of the West Coast. The prairie fire of golf in the last two decades has not missed out on Nigeria, where despite all the physical difficulties of climate and terrain there are over a dozen courses and a growing army of golfers. Tony Fisher has fanned the flames by annual coaching missions to Lagos and other centres in recent years. Each time his visits have lasted a little longer until his leave of absence from Sudbury has stretched to as much as eight weeks. . . . 'In response to popular demand,' chuckles Tony, the man who gets a laugh out of practically everything he does.

Fisher came back from Africa one spring to win the Sunningdale Foursomes with Mrs. Marley Spearman, twice British women's champion. Partnering that great competitor Marley was the first reason Tony gave for his success. Two months in Nigeria was the other. 'I must have been the only British pro who had played golf every day of the year up to Sunningdale at the end of March,' he said. 'The sun on your back cannot do anything but good for your game. When I used to winter at home there was more than half the time when to go out and practise in icy weather did your swing more harm than good.'

Tony was ready to talk and talk about his African adventure. His enthusiasm for the trip was not based upon what it had done for his own game, but on what he had done for other golfers. Then that is the kind of man he is. It is not for nothing that Sudbury club conferred the signal honour of honorary membership upon him after only two years' service as their professional.

Typical of him is his volunteer work among the African boy caddies of the Ikoyi Club, Nigeria's largest club, at Lagos, the capital. On his second visit in 1963 Fisher started a caddies' tournament which is contested each year out there. He teaches the boys in mass clinics sandwiched between his full and strenuous programme of teaching and playing with the local members—the prime purpose of his presence in Nigeria. It is done by lopping an hour off his 12.30 to 3 break from the midday sun.

At Ikoyi there are 150 caddie boys who spend half their day caddying and the other half at classes serving apprenticeships at trades such as electricians, building or carpentry.

'The "boys" are organised for the club by the caddie-masters,' said Fisher. 'Why I am so enthusiastic about the boys is the fantastic keenness they show for the game of golf. The scores in their tournament are much better each year. Their techniques have improved so much. They are at the stage I was as a youngster, full of ambitions in the game.

'It gives me a great kick to think that there in a country a long way off from us, and with a totally different way of life, are these lads playing golf because of me. One cannot say just how far it will develop, but the day could come when Nigeria produces its own professionals. They would come from this school of caddies. A start is being made, in fact. The winner of the caddies' tournament for two years has been a lad called Young Dick, and the Ikoyi Club have promoted him from caddying to playing with the members.'

No wonder that to the caddie boys of Lagos Arnold Palmer might not exist. Their hero is Tony Fisher, who took an interest in them from his first visit, gave them clubs to practise with, and the Tony Fisher Cup to compete for. They in turn gave him a native chieftain's dress called an *agbada*, an honour usually reserved for a high-ranking, long-service European official. Another year he brought home from them a huge ebony elephant, and on a later visit yet another native robe. The day could come when Tony is referred to as 'the father of Nigerian professional golf'.

Fisher once went to gaol while in Nigeria—as a visitor. He went to see the man who was responsible for his winter migrations. This was Chief Enaharu, a Nigerian diplomat who became a member of Sudbury while in London and had the idea of introducing Fisher to the Ikoyi Club. The Chief was a political prisoner.

Tony could never have dreamt as he set off for his first trip in January 1962 of the massive programme he would be undertaking four years later. In an eight-week spell in Africa he gives no less than 300 lessons and plays 50 rounds of golf. The original arrangement was to coach at Lagos. This has grown to an engagement that covers three other big clubs—Port Harcourt, with a 13-hole course, Enugu, a coal-mining centre with a 12-hole course, and Ibadan, the second biggest city with an 18-hole course.

'While out there I do a 12-hour day, with the usual breaks, and a seven-day week, apart from the odd day off,' Tony said. 'Teaching starts at 7.30 and lasts until 12.30, with a half-hour break. I play a fourball every afternoon at three. In effect I am the professional to the four clubs while I am there. The advantage is that the appointment book is full all the time and as it is the dry season we have no interruptions by the weather.

'The pupils vary from single-figure players to complete beginners. I think the only nationality I did not teach were Russians. Japanese, Americans, Nigerians, and people from almost every country in Europe were there. Naturally, language is a problem. I don't speak any Japanese, and they don't speak much English. Teaching becomes a miming contest. I show them their faults—the wrong way. Then I show them the right way.

'Demonstration and Imitation, I suppose you could call it. It is as good a way as any, really. Words are inclined to confuse golf instruction. Although they have no professionals out there, the beginners are started off by the good players holding clinics. You know how it is—golfers will always help each other. Some, of course, I start off myself. The membership is always turning over as people finish their tours of duty. The fundamentals are grip and stance. I see that they are holding the club properly and standing properly—without that there is no swing.'

Is golf a different game in the tropics? 'The major difference is that you putt on "browns", instead of greens. This, and the nature of the fairways in the dry season, makes the short game totally different,' Tony explains.

'Browns' are a smoothly rolled surface mixture of sand and oil, on a hard base. They are all circular and quite small in size. Because of their true, consistent surface and the size you are looking for single putts every time you are on the brown. The cups are up at surface level, so anything banged at the back of the hole will not do—it will jump out. Putts have to be just the right strength. Pitching on to the browns is out, of course. You can put your wedge away. The approach shot has to be a run-up with a five- or six-iron, or the club Tony Fisher has introduced for the shot—'The Scuffler', the old-time jigger in modern dress.

Lagos in the rainy season has fairways as lush as you will find, but when Fisher is there the grass is very sparse and the surface is mostly sand. 'It is like playing a long bunker shot. You have to take the ball clean. Hit on the upswing,' he said.

Nigeria is predominantly a British market for clubs and balls. Top-grade balls are 5s. 9d. in the stores or 4s. 6d. at the clubs, who buy them direct. Clubs are roughly the same price as in Britain, import duty balancing our purchase tax. They are sold in the stores and imported by the clubs as well.

The clubs are not purely golf clubs, but complete recreational organisations on country club lines, with facilities for tennis, squash, badminton, swimming and other sports as well as the golf course. Ikoyi, the largest club, in Lagos, has a total membership of 2,500, of which the golf section is 750 strong. To fill the course rapidly there are starting points at the first, seventh and 13th holes.

A sample winter for Tony is a fortnight at Lagos, four weeks divided between three other clubs, and, to finish, a final 12 days in Lagos. He flies the 500 miles from Lagos to Port Harcourt, where rainstorms give the course green fairways all the year. He goes on by air to Enugu and then Ibadan, and returns to Lagos by road. He has a large American car at his disposal all the time, and is put up privately by club members.

His favourite local rule is one they'll never have to make at Sudbury—a free pick is allowed from anthills. The only other peculiar local hazard is that the courses are cut out of thick bush and jungle.

'If you knock one off the course you are stone dead,' Tony said. 'Fortunately the fairways are wide. There would be no point in making tiger courses where the members play solely for enjoyment.

'The courses are full every day of the week, because many offices work from eight o'clock till two, straight through, and others finish at four in the afternoon. They'd never get them round the course if they did not give them plenty of room.'

Fisher does his teaching and playing at shade temperatures of 90 to 95 degrees, and up to 85 per cent humidity. But he suffered no ill-effects, had no problems of diet . . . 'Most of the food we ate is imported except for the plentiful supplies of fresh oranges, grapefruit and pineapples.' It is pretty obvious that Tony Fisher is a good traveller, as well as being a tremendous flag-waver for Britain's professional golfers.

Being a one-man coaching ambassador to Africa is, however, just one facet of Tony's golfing life. As a club pro he is a personality in his own right. He allies to a happy, friendly outlook a first-class grounding in the profession he was tossed into by his environment. London-born Tony—July 25th, 1933—found himself growing up on the Moor Park course at the age of 12 because his parents worked there as steward and stewardess. At 14 he was a Moor Park Artisans member, playing to scratch. He thought nothing of rising at six in the morning to play nine holes before school. He caddied enthusiastically at week-ends, and was selected by the club's best players.

When told that his week-end caddying barred his entry for the well-known Moor Park boys' classic, the Carris Trophy, a shattered and discouraged Tony made up his mind that the only future for him lay in being a professional golfer. His first job was with the late Cliff Henry at Pinner Hill. He had a spell on the Northwood greenstaff and then moved on to Hartsbourne Country Club under Pat Keene, the junior of a crack assistants team which included Harry Weetman and Tony Harman. Then came National Service; a short spell at Estoril in Portugal, with Pat Keene; marriage at the age of 20; and a job back home with Harry Weetman at Croham Hurst.

He was then invited back to Hartsbourne with the Hunt family when they moved from Atherstone in Warwickshire. There Tony fell ill and was out of golf for 18 months with a chest complaint. 'All that time the Hartsbourne members looked after me. I owe them a great debt,' says Fisher. In December '57 came the final move—to Sudbury as assistant to Dave Thomas. When Dave went as playing professional to Sunningdale Fisher was at once appointed his successor. The club looked no further, the job was not advertised. 'I regard that as a great compliment,' said Tony.

The outstanding relationship between club and pro was cemented two years ago when Fisher was made an honorary member of Sudbury. Plainly he gives his club the kind of service beyond the call of normal duty. I asked, 'What is your attitude to the club pro's job?'

'Simply that I work for every one of the members. There are little things I do beyond that, which they don't expect,' he said. These 'little things' include making it a duty to go and support any Sudbury players engaged in matches or tournaments. Even to changing a wheel for someone who has an unexpected flat tyre while out on the course. Service with a king-size smile is the slogan of the well-liked 'Fish', as he is affectionately called at the club, and by his fellow pros.

Back in 1962 he was a semi-finalist in the News of the World at Walton Heath. He rates himself a far better golfer now. 'I was the kind of player who'd play 14 holes perfectly and have two or three out bounds or something equally silly at the others. Now I have learned that you have to keep the ball on the course for 18 holes. If I get the feeling that I am not going to hit a fairway I'll take an iron. I feel that if any crisis crops up on the course I can deal with it much better.

'The biggest improvement in my game, though, is holing out. It is something that I have worked and worked at. Not only the action, but the mental attitude. In the last nine months I have holed more putts at crucial stages than ever I have before. This was happening at the end of last season. It is positive thinking, I suppose you'd call it. That the putt is going in the hole. Don't think of lagging up.'

To this improved outlook Fisher allies the controlled three-quarter swing that a big man can afford. He has 18 st. to help propel the ball, and powerful hands to match. It is quite conceivable that he will indeed make an impact on the tournament scene. Whether he does or not he will still remain one of the personalities of the professional golf world, winning an ever-widening circle of friends beyond the confines of Sudbury Club, Middlesex county, and the far-flung fairways of Nigeria.

WITHDRAWN